DEEP PRAYER

Prayer that Pursues Intimacy with God

STEVE MATTEUCCI

Deep Prayer
Copyright © 2024 by Stephen J. Matteucci

All rights reserved. No part of this publication may be reproduced, stored in a retrieval system, or transmitted in any form by any means, electronic, mechanical, photocopy, recording, or otherwise, without the prior permission of the copyright holder, except as provided for by USA copyright law.

Unless otherwise noted, all quotations from the Bible are from The Holy Bible, English Standard Version, copyright © 2001 by Crossway, a publishing ministry of Good News Publishers. Used by permission. All rights reserved. Italics within Scripture quotations indicate emphasis added by the author.

Paperback ISBN: 979-8-9915801-2-0

Library of Congress Control Number: 2024920288

Cover Design by Lou Designs

To my wife, Lisa, who taught me everything I know about being in a deep and intimate relationship.

And to my children, Mark, Abigail, and Joe, who showed me just how much a father can love his children.

TABLE OF CONTENTS

Acknowledgements	vii
Introduction	1
Chapter 1: The Definition of Deep Prayer	9
Chapter 2: The Model of Deep Prayer	40
Chapter 3: The Relationship of Deep Prayer	57
Chapter 4: The Language of Deep Prayer	83
Chapter 5: The Blessing of Deep Prayer	123
Chapter 6: The Conversation of Deep Prayer	147
Chapter 7: The End of Deep Prayer	178
A Call to Deep Prayer	201
Epilogue	206

ACKNOWLEDGEMENTS

The book you are holding records my conclusions from a long journey of prayer. Through decade after decade of my Christian life, I didn't just pray, I also wanted to understand prayer itself. I wanted to know the answers to some basic questions: What kind of prayer does God answer? What is the proper way to talk to the God of the universe? What prayer requests are acceptable to God? After a while, I got to the more philosophical questions: If God knows everything, why am I telling him things? If God is perfect, how can my feeble prayers change him? If God has a plan (whatever that looks like), what impact can my prayers have on the world? I tried hard to answer these questions, but I always knew there was something missing. Eventually, I got to the heart of the matter and started asking the central questions: Why did God invent prayer? Why does God listen to prayer? What is his goal for my prayers? I wrote this book to share my answers to these central questions, to show you the ultimate goal—the most important reason—that you take time out of your busy day, find a quiet spot, and talk to the supreme being, the sovereign Lord, the great God of the universe.

There are some people I want to thank for walking along with me as I asked these questions and wrote this book. Yasar Makram is my dear friend, with whom I have had regular conversations about God, the universe, and other things. He is a deep thinker and has challenged me regularly to reassess my assumptions and conclusions. My former pastor, Greg Gilbert, read a manuscript of an early version of this book and his comments helped narrow and clarify the focus of its message.

Matt Jacobs has been my faithful editor through all the versions and revisions of this book. Matt is an attorney who can smell a bad argument, a non-sequitur, and a rabbit trail from miles away. He delighted in showing me where I skipped steps in logic, when I was obsessing over minor points, and when I was talking to myself instead of to you. He was tough, he was mean, he was sarcastic, and he was faithful. This book is far better because of his work and, if you find something unclear or too wordy, it's probably because I didn't listen to Matt.

Finally, my wife, Lisa, taught me everything I know about being in a relationship and has shaped my thinking more than anyone else. Before I married her, I loved learning for the sake of learning and would be easily enthralled by an elegant theory that had no connection to real life. Lisa was the opposite: she could never be seduced by mere theory. She wanted to know how deep truths helped solve the real problems of a life lived out in a complex and confusing world. Through many conversations over four decades, she has taught me to be a much more practical thinker. And she, more than anyone else, has heard me talk about prayer as I asked my basic questions and my philosophical questions, until I finally made it around to the central questions. She read what I thought was the final manuscript of this book and did what she has always done: asked hard questions, shared her wise insights, and made supremely practical suggestions. I am very thankful that God sent Lisa to me and that I have had the privilege of living life with her.

Steve Matteucci
September 2024

INTRODUCTION

Shortly after I became a Christian, someone took me aside and told me that Christians pray, so I started praying. I still remember the first time I got down on my knees, how I was lifted up to heaven, how I was ushered into the presence of God himself, how I was able to speak to him face-to-face, how I was able to make my petitions right there before his throne.

Just kidding.

The truth is, I didn't know what I was doing. I was young (barely a teenager), I was inexperienced, and I was self-centered. On top of all that, I wasn't very good at making conversation with people I could see and hear so, sitting in the dark, all alone, and trying to talk to the invisible God wasn't easy.

Other Christians helped me, my church taught me, I read some books, and eventually I became more comfortable and more consistent talking to God. But I still had a problem—a much bigger problem, in fact. While I was learning to pray, I was also reading the Bible and what I read in the Bible about prayer didn't match my own experience. At all. So, I read books about Christians through the centuries who prayed over their lifetimes and found that those testimonies didn't line up with my own prayer life. At all. So, I observed the more mature Christians around me and paid attention to their public prayers, in church services, to open Sunday School classes, even before a meal, and my own experience even fell short of that. I knew something was wrong with me, but I had no idea what it was or how to fix it.

What I found in the Bible made me feel like a failure, as I read about amazing and miraculous answers to prayer that put my feeble requests to shame. Elijah prayed on Mt. Carmel and fire came down from heaven to vindicate God's name (1Kings 18:17-40). After Hezekiah prayed, the invading Syrian army was killed during the night (2 Kings 19). Joshua prayed and the sun stayed out for a whole day (Joshua 10:12-14). Meanwhile, I was praying small prayers with mundane requests about parochial problems that, even when God answered, the changes were barely noticed (even by me).

If that wasn't bad enough, I also read the most astonishing promises about prayer that didn't match up with my experience. For example, during the Last Supper, Jesus told his disciples, "Whatever you ask in my name, this I will do, that the Father may be glorified in the Son. If you ask me anything in my name, I will do it" (John 14:13-14). Later that evening, he doubled down and made this promise: "If you abide in me, and my words abide in you, ask whatever you wish, and it will be done for you" (John 15:7). A little

Introduction

later he *tripled* down: "In that day you will ask nothing of me. Truly, truly, I say to you, whatever you ask of the Father in my name, he will give it to you. Until now you have asked nothing in my name. Ask, and you will receive, that your joy may be full" (John 16:23-24). Years before that supper, Jesus told the crowd listening to his Sermon on the Mount, "Ask, and it will be given to you; seek, and you will find; knock, and it will be opened to you. For everyone who asks receives, and the one who seeks finds, and to the one who knocks it will be opened" (Matthew 7:7-8). Then Jesus told his disciples,

> Have faith in God. Truly, I say to you, whoever says to this mountain, 'Be taken up and thrown into the sea,' and does not doubt in his heart, but believes that what he says will come to pass, it will be done for him. Therefore I tell you, whatever you ask in prayer, believe that you have received it, and it will be yours" (Mark 11:22-24).

Five promises all saying that if I asked God for something, he would give it to me. Sure, there were conditions: I had to ask in Jesus's name, I had to abide in Jesus, Jesus's words had to abide in me, and I had to have faith. But I was sincerely trying to meet those conditions, not just to get my prayers answered, but to grow as a Christian, and yet my prayers still seemed so small and often went unanswered.

By the grace and mercy of God, I didn't give up praying and I didn't water down those astonishing promises to line up with my pathetic experience. Instead, I kept reading the Bible, started studying theology, poured over biblical commentaries, and devoured lots of books about prayer. I wanted to understand prayer. I wanted to know how prayer worked. I wanted to see prayer from God's perspective. I was like the guy working on a puzzle who didn't have all the pieces. They weren't in the box, they were lost all around the house. Every once in a while I would find a new piece and fit it carefully into the big picture. Slowly, the pieces started to come together and I could see the picture more clearly. After several decades, I finally understood why God wants us to pray, what kinds of things we should pray for, and how to talk to the infinite God. All these puzzle pieces and all these lessons over all these years had made a beautiful, complex, and detailed picture that I have entitled, Deep Prayer. What I call deep prayers are not more intense or more theological prayers, but prayers prayed with a deeper purpose.

    Now, as someone who had stared at small, disjointed puzzle pieces for so long, seeing this big picture was exciting! It was exciting because I saw something glorious in that big picture. I saw that, in deep prayer, we unload our heaviest burdens; in deep prayer, we express our greatest joys; in deep prayer, we repent of our worst sins; in deep prayer, we are freed from those sins. In deep prayer, we see God more clearly, we look at the world more carefully, and we examine our souls more closely. In deep prayer, we're

Introduction

more grateful to our Father, more satisfied in Jesus, more connected to the Holy Spirit. Deep prayers engage our soul, while shallow prayers put us to sleep; deep prayers flow from desire, while shallow prayers perform a duty; deep prayers are steady and consistent, while shallow prayers are sporadic and intermittent.

I wrote this book to help Christians pray deep prayers to God regularly and intentionally.

That's my mission statement and you will hear it over and over in different forms throughout the book. Unfortunately, all the words in my mission statement have been relentlessly under attack throughout Western culture for my whole life. If you've been influenced by these attacks, then you might not have the same definition of these words that I'm using. So, I want to start off by defining my terms clearly for you. The way I define these words here in this introduction is the only way I use them throughout this book.

Let's start off with the easiest ones: **regularly and intentionally**. I know that, once a person becomes a Christian (as defined below) and starts praying (as defined below), God (as defined below) draws that Christian into deep (as defined below) prayer with him. So, I know you pray deep prayers to God. I didn't write this book because I think that none your prayers are deep or that you will never pray a deep prayer until you have absorbed the lessons of this book and put them into practice. But, unless you know what makes a prayer deep, your deep prayers will be sporadic, passive, and accidental. That's where the words "regularly and intentionally" come in. My mission is to help you pray deep prayers every time you pray, as an active pursuit. Since God wants you to pray deeply to him, I want to help you pray deep prayers to God regularly and intentionally.

Next, when I use the word **Christian** in this book, I am referring to a person who has had a very specific kind of experience. I'm not referring to anyone who attends a church or to all people who are not Muslims or Hindus or atheists. In this book, the word Christian means a person whose soul has been regenerated by the Holy Spirit, who has seen the reality and seriousness of his or her sin, who has recognized that he or she is a rebel against God, who has repented of known sin, who has trusted in the finished work of Jesus Christ on the cross for forgiveness and salvation, and who has been adopted by God the Father into his family. While this definition may be specific, it certainly isn't narrow. A Christian can be any kind of person—young or old, rich or poor, male or female, from any country, speaking any language, with any skin color, living in any culture, attending any kind of church. The beauty of the biblical definition of a Christian is that it demolishes every barrier that our world erects between people and says that the only

Introduction

difference that matters is whether you've been adopted by God as his child or are in rebellion against God as his enemy.

This is a book about prayer, so now I need to define what I mean by the words **pray** and **prayer**. I have a very simple definition of prayer: Prayer is a conversation with God. Prayer is not emptying the mind of all thoughts to create a clearer headspace or sending happy feelings out into the universe on behalf of people we know. Prayer is actively and thoughtfully conversing with God. It's both a spiritual activity and a rational activity, as Paul wrote, "I will pray with my spirit, but I will pray with my mind also" (1 Corinthians 14:15). It's a conversation because, in prayer, we also listen to God. The words of God are given to us in the Bible. During prayer, God may fill our minds with thoughts, ideas, and wisdom, but they all are connected to and dependent on the words God has revealed and recorded in the Bible. We will see more about how this conversation works later in the book.

The word **God** has been under relentless attack throughout my lifetime in an attempt to erase all uniqueness and all personality out of the word. So, Allah is called God and Buddha is called God and the many idols around the world are referred to as Gods. This means the God Christians worship is not unique, he is just one of many. Then they will tell us that we all have the spark of the divine in us and assign divine attributes to impersonal things, like the weather or science or nature. Once again, I reject all those fuzzy definitions and turn to the pages of Scripture. When I use the word God in this book, I am referring to the one and only God who has a single divine nature that is shared by three distinct persons, the Father, the Son, and the Holy Spirit, who indwell one another in a perfect relationship of love and unity. God is a Trinity, and his unique nature as the Triune God is supremely important to deep prayer.

That leaves us with the word **deep**, a key word for this book that requires a whole chapter to define. First, I'll share part of my journey toward deep prayer by showing you the various ways I have tried to distinguish between good and bad (or acceptable and unacceptable or proper and improper) prayers. Then I will show the key element that makes a prayer deep. Finally, I will demonstrate from Scripture that what I am calling deep prayer is the kind of prayer God wants us to pray to him. So, let's move on to chapter one.

Chapter 1

The Definition of Deep Prayer

When I was a boy, my parents joined a YMCA outdoor pool each summer. This was a big, public pool with lots of kids swimming in it every minute it was open. To keep small children and bad swimmers safe, the lifeguards were very strict about who could swim in the deep end and who had to stay in the shallow end. The first step toward enforcing this life-and-death rule was to run a bright blue rope, with lots of big blue and white floats, across the pool to divide the deep end from the shallow end. You cannot tell kids to stay in the shallow end if you fail to mark the start of the deep end. The same is true of praying deep prayers. How can I tell you to pray deep prayers if I cannot draw a clear line between the deep end and the shallow end? Unless I draw the line between the deep and the shallow clearly and biblically, you will not know which side of the line your prayers are on or how to cross over into the deep end. I know from long experience that the line isn't easy to find. Let me share with you some of the lines I have tried to draw between the deep and the shallow over my 50 years of praying.

DEEP PRAYER

My First Line: Answered vs. Unanswered

I still remember the first line I drew between a good prayer and a bad prayer (I wasn't thinking about deep and shallow back then). I assumed that a good prayer was answered by God and a bad prayer went unanswered. When I was a teenager and a new Christian, back in the mid-1970's, I became fascinated by prayer after reading a book about how God miraculously and powerfully answered the prayers of his people in both the Bible and church history. Unfortunately, my first thought wasn't, "Wow! God is really amazing!" it was, "Wow! How can I get that kind of power to work for me!" I started imagining all the things I could get God to do for me in this world just by developing a habit of prayer. So, I read every book about prayer I could get my hands on, focusing my time, energy, and attention on how to get answers to my prayers from God. I wanted to find the secret key that would unlock the windows of heaven and get me what I was asking for.

So, without realizing what I was doing, I drew my line between answered prayers and unanswered prayers.

However, the line between the deep and the shallow (or even the good and the bad) cannot possibly be drawn there, for two very good reasons. The first reason is practical. If a deep prayer is one God answers, then we cannot know if a prayer is deep until God either answers the prayer or until circumstances make it clear that God is not going to answer it. Decades could pass, making it impossible for us to use

The Definition of Deep Prayer

this line to regularly and intentionally pray deep prayers. The second reason is biblical. There are some amazingly deep prayers recorded in the Bible that God did not answer.

When the great Israelite King, David, was strong and secure in his kingdom, he decided he was above the law—even the law of God—and committed adultery with a woman named Bathsheba (2 Samuel 11). When Bathsheba informed the king that she was pregnant with his child, David tried to cover up his sin, first by calling her husband home from war so that he would sleep with his wife (and everyone would assume he was the father) and then, when that didn't work, arranging for her husband to be killed in battle and marrying Bathsheba immediately (so everyone would assume the child was conceived after they had been married).

David fooled a lot of people with his cover up, but he couldn't fool God. God sent Nathan the prophet to David to tell him that God had seen all his sin (the adultery and the cover up) and that one of the consequences of his sin would be that his baby boy would die (2 Samuel 12:1-14). When the child became sick, David fasted and prayed to God for a week, pleading with God for the child's life (2 Samuel 12:15-16; 22). Part of what David prayed during that week is recorded for us as 115:51, a deep prayer of repentance (I will explain how we know this is a deep prayer a little later). Despite these deep prayers, the child died. David's prayer for the child was not answered.

DEEP PRAYER

In 2 Corinthians 12, Paul wrote that God had given him a thorn in his flesh to harass him and keep him from becoming conceited because of the amazing revelations that he had seen (vv. 1-7). Whatever that thorn was, Paul didn't like it, so he "pleaded with the Lord about this, that it should leave" him (v. 8). But the Lord refused to answer Paul's prayers, telling him instead that "My grace is sufficient for you, for my power is made perfect in weakness" (v. 9). Despite his deep prayers, Paul would have to learn to live with this thorn rather than having it removed in answer to his prayers.

On the night Jesus was arrested by his enemies, he went to the Garden of Gethsemane with his disciples. During those few hours before the Jews arrested him, he prayed to his Father, asking if he could avoid going to the cross. The prayers Jesus prayed in that garden are the deepest prayers recorded in the Bible. The way Jesus prayed in the garden that night is the model of deep prayer on which this book is based. But, just like David and Paul, Jesus's deep prayers went unanswered by his Father and Jesus ended up enduring the pain he prayed to avoid.

None of these unanswered prayers are criticized in the Bible; in fact, they are commended to us. Therefore, wherever we end up drawing the line between the deep and the shallow, it has to explain how an unanswered prayer can be deep.

My Unconscious Line: Others vs. Myself

The Bible is filled with exhortations, instructions, and warnings to put other people ahead of ourselves. Just think about the biblical theme of love, for an example. Love is inherently others-centered and throughout the New Testament we're commanded to love one another.[1] Another way of saying this is, "love your neighbor as yourself."[2] Jesus even commands us to love our enemies (Matthew 5:43). The Bible also reinforces this theme of others-centeredness by warning us against selfishness and pride, which are both inherently self-centered. Paul wrote to the Philippians, "Do nothing from selfish ambition or conceit, but in humility count others more significant than yourselves. Let each of you look not only to his own interests, but also to the interests of others" (Philippians 2:3-4). He then used the humble selflessness of Jesus's Incarnation and crucifixion as the example to follow (vv. 5-8).

---

[1] John 13:34-35; 15:12, 17; Romans 12:10; Ephesians 4:2; Hebrews 10:24; 1 Peter 1:22; 4:8; 1 John 3:11, 23; 4:7, 11-12.
[2] Leviticus 19:18; Matthew 22:39; Romans 13:9; Galatians 5:14; James 2:8.

Having been steeped in this biblical teaching over my Christian life, there was a time when I hesitated to pray for myself, unconsciously assuming that it's always better to pray for others. Deep prayers, then, were intercessory prayers that asked God to help others, not prayers centered on the things I needed or wanted.

However, the line between deep and shallow prayers cannot be drawn here, either. Yes, you can pray deep prayers for others, but you can also pray shallow prayers for others. And yes, you can easily pray shallow prayers for yourself, but you can also pray deep prayers for yourself. Remember, the prayer that I have identified as the deepest recorded in the entire Bible was a prayer Jesus prayed for himself. The greatest missionary who ever walked the earth prayed a deep prayer for his thorn in the flesh to be removed. On top of those examples, every prayer by any Christian who repents of his or her sins and asks God's forgiveness is a prayer for him or herself, not for anyone else.

The Bible records and commends many prayers that people prayed for themselves and their own needs. Therefore, wherever we end up drawing the line between the deep and the shallow, it has to explain how a prayer for yourself can still be deep.

My Language Line: Eloquent vs. Inarticulate

How did you learn to pray?

The Definition of Deep Prayer

Think about those early, awkward sessions of prayer you had. There you were, sitting alone in a room, trying to talk to someone you couldn't see or hear. What are you supposed to say to God? What's the proper protocol when talking to God? What kind of language is acceptable to God? It's a struggle. But you go to church and you hear other people pray: in a prayer meeting, during the Sunday morning service, to open a Sunday School class, before eating a meal. Since these are mature Christians who have been praying for years, you naturally assume they know what's right and wrong and so you start your own prayer journey by imitating them.

I'm old enough that the prayers I heard in church were prayed in the King's English—King James, that is. I heard formal and flowery prayers addressing God as "Thee" and "Thou" and "Thy," as in "Thou art great and we love Thee for Thy greatness." Then, as I read the Bible, I came across prayers that were literary masterpieces, with intricately woven language and even a poetic cadence.

With that kind of experience, it was easy for me to assume that a deep prayer was formal and eloquent, while a shallow prayer must be common and base. God is a great King, and you do not talk to a king the way you talk to other commoners.

But you cannot draw the line between deep prayers and shallow prayers by evaluating the eloquence of the presentation. For every eloquent and poetic prayer in the

DEEP PRAYER

Bible, there are also plenty that are blunt and rough. One of the deepest prayers in the Old Testament, prayed by the great Moses himself, consists of only five simple words: "Please, show me your glory" (Exodus 33:18). In Psalm 88, we read these blunt words addressed to God: "O LORD, why do you cast my soul away? Why do you hide your face from me?" (v. 14). After Israel suffered defeat in battle, the Sons of Korah prayed a prayer that included these harsh words: "But you have rejected us and disgraced us and have not gone out with our armies. You have made us turn back from the foe, and those who hate us have gotten spoil" (Psalm 44:9-10). Job asked God to stay away from him and let him die: "I loathe my life; I would not live forever. Leave me alone, for my days are a breath. What is man, that you make so much of him, and that you set your heart on him, visit him every morning and test him every moment?" (Job 7:16-18). Habakkuk questioned God's wisdom in sending the Babylonians to punish Israel's sins: "You who are of purer eyes than to see evil and cannot look at wrong, why do you idly look at traitors and remain silent when the wicked swallows up the man more righteous than he?" (Habakkuk 1:13).

I had read these verses many times, not isolated like this but in their contexts, surrounded by other carefully written words, so it was easy for me to miss the bluntness, the audacity, and the rashness being expressed in these deep prayers. But then, when I was able to listen to these prayers

The Definition of Deep Prayer

objectively, the bluntness, audacity, and rashness were there. Then I remembered what Paul wrote in Romans 8:26. In that verse, Paul encouraged his readers by explaining that, even when they didn't know what to pray for, "the Spirit himself intercedes for us with groanings *too deep for words*."

Whatever makes a prayer deep, it's not the eloquence of the words we use. In fact, it's sometimes the inability to speak at all.

The Social Media Line: Happy vs. Sad

The technology we use every day shapes the way we live our lives. This has been true of all technology, from the movable type printing press to the steam locomotive to the internal combustion engine to the telephone to the television to the computer. As technology weaves its way into our daily routine, we find ourselves subtlety changing how we live, how we work, even how we think. A lot of these changes have been helpful and have had positive effects in the lives of people. Other changes have been harmful and, sometimes over a long period of time, show up as a net negative for people.

The technology I'm worried about here is social media. I know people use social media in good ways, ways that connect them to family and friends so they can keep relationships from drifting apart. But the negative effects of social media keep popping up. The one I'm thinking of here, the one that could impact your practice of prayer, is your ability to present yourself on social media in whatever way you choose, your ability to curate your life to make yourself look as good as you can. The goal isn't to show the world who you really are: what you struggle with, what causes you pain, what weaknesses you have, where your character flaws are hidden, or even what your true opinions are. The goal is to show the world the image of yourself that you want it to see. If this use of social media becomes a habit that shapes your view of yourself and the world, then you could start to be uncomfortable in your relationships out in the real world. Even worse, you could carry those habits into your prayers.

If prayer becomes the time you upload to God the best version of yourself that you can create—the one you think he will approve of most—then you may start thinking that happy, positive prayers are better than sad or negative prayers. I actually drew this line long before social media was invented because, based on my own reading of the Bible, I thought that these were the deepest prayers. After all, James told us to "Count it all joy . . . when you meet trials of various kinds" (James 1:2); and Paul said, "we rejoice in our sufferings" (Romans 5:3), and he told the Colossians, "Now I rejoice in my sufferings for your sake" (Colossians 1:24). We're even commanded to "rejoice always, pray without ceasing, give thanks in all circumstances; for this is the will of God in Christ Jesus for you" (1Thessalonians 5:16-18). Anyone, I thought, can whine to God about their

The Definition of Deep Prayer

struggles and pain, but clearly the deeper prayer would be to show him how you can rejoice and thank him for everything.

Prayers of praise and thanksgiving should be an important part of your prayers and, yes, they can be some of the deepest prayers you ever pray. The psalms are filled with prayers of praise and thanksgiving[3] and Paul regularly expressed his thanks to God for the Christians and the churches he ministered to.[4] So, I'm not suggesting that praises are not an important part of Christian prayer. All I'm saying right now is that praises are not inherently deeper kinds of prayers than intercession or even complaints.

Alongside prayers of great praise, the psalms are also filled with prayers of complaint to God, in language that expresses many different emotions: anger, frustration, disappointment, confusion, and sadness. In fact, there are so many of these (about a third of the total) that they have their own category. Theologians refer to these as the Lament Psalms, and these kinds of prayers are not restricted to the Psalms. Many of Job's prayers in his book are laments; a lot of the prayers Habakkuk prays in his book are laments; and

---

[3] I mean "filled." There are too many verses to try to list them out and, by listing a representative sample, I might give the impression that the number is smaller than it is. Instead, open your Bible to the book of Psalms and start leafing through the pages. You will find plenty of examples there.

[4] There are a lot of these, too. Flip through the letters of Paul and you will find them in almost every letter he wrote to churches (Galatians is a notable exception).

there is an entire book written by Jeremiah called Lamentations.

These prayers are remarkably deep in ways we modern Christians, shaped by our social media habits, have a hard time grasping. If you have conditioned yourself to focus on only the happy parts of your life, the language in the lament prayers will sound strange to you (and by "strange" I mean "wrong"). I haven't given you my definition of a deep prayer yet, but when I do, you will see that laments are indispensable to praying deeply. So, I'm not merely saying that laments can be deep prayers, I'm saying you cannot regularly and intentionally pray deep prayers without them.

The Most Popular Line: Spiritual vs. Material

When Christians consciously draw the line between good and bad prayers, I think most make a distinction between prayers that ask God for spiritual and eternal things and prayers that ask God for physical and material things. In fact, I remember being a member of a church whose elders were concerned about the shallowness of our congregational prayer meetings and sent an e-mail to the members asking us to consider bringing deeper requests to these meetings. In their e-mail, these elders strongly implied that praying for physical and materials needs was shallow and praying for spiritual concerns was deep. Our prayer meetings, they said, had become dominated by the physical and material (just like prayer meetings of most churches across all

The Definition of Deep Prayer

denominations): My mom was admitted to the hospital and no one seems to know what's wrong; the kids are sick this week; brother Joe twisted his ankle and will be laid up for a while; our dear sister Mary has been feeling light-headed and is concerned; my job has been a real hassle lately; I have a big test coming up in school; the car broke down yesterday; I have a crucial decision to make about my career and need some guidance.

I remember reading that e-mail and agreeing with my elders on the distinction between the shallow end and the deep end of the prayer pool. I can even show you an incident from the ministry of Jesus where he seemed to draw the line in exactly the same place. In John 6, a large crowd followed Jesus up a mountain, where he was sitting with his disciples (vv. 3-5), and Jesus fed the entire crowd with the equivalent of a handful of dinner rolls (vv. 9-11). The next day, the crowd went searching for Jesus (Jesus had walked across the Sea of Galilee during the night). When Jesus saw all these eager, motivated followers, he said to them:

> Truly, truly, I say to you, you are seeking me, not because you saw signs, but because you ate your fill of the loaves. Do not work for the food that perishes, but for the food that endures to eternal life, which the Son of Man will give to you. For on him God the Father has set his seal (vv. 26-28).

Jesus perceived that these people were not seeking him because they realized, after seeing his great miracle, that

DEEP PRAYER

Jesus was the long-awaited Messiah come to Israel, but because they had been given one free meal and they wanted to have another. They were not seeking food that endures to eternal life, but food that perishes. In this rebuke, Jesus himself seemed to teach that asking him for physical and material things is shallow and asking him for spiritual and eternal things is deep.

If that's not enough evidence, the Bible records many prayers that ask God for spiritual and eternal blessings, rather than physical and material blessings. Paul sprinkles these kinds of spiritual prayers throughout his letters to different churches. He prayed that the Ephesians would have "the eyes of [their] hearts enlightened" (1:18), "to know the love of Christ" (3:19), and to be "filled with all the fullness of God" (3:19). His prayer for the Philippians was for their "love to abound more and more" (1:9) and that they would be "filled with the fruit of righteousness that comes through Jesus Christ" (1:11). He asked God that the Colossians would be filled with the knowledge of God's will in all spiritual wisdom and understanding (1:9). He prayed for the Thessalonians that the Lord would make them "increase and abound in love for one another and for all" (1 Thessalonians 3:12) and that God would make them "worthy of his calling and . . . fulfill every resolve for good and every work of faith by his power" (2 Thessalonians 1:11). Paul prayed spiritual prayers for the people in these churches.

The Definition of Deep Prayer

Examples like this compel us to the conclusion that deep prayers ask God for spiritual things, while shallow prayers ask God to meet physical and material needs.

But before we injure ourselves jumping to that conclusion, we should consider some other passages. For example, when Jesus's disciples asked him for a lesson in prayer, Jesus gave them a model prayer to help them. Embedded in that prayer was the request, "Give us this day our daily bread" (Matthew 6:11). This was a prayer for God to supply them with food every day—like when he gave manna to the Israelites wandering in the desert—a prayer to meet a physical need with a material substance. You could, of course, argue that this is still a spiritual prayer because it's surrounded by spiritual and eternal requests—for God's name, God's kingdom, God's will, God's forgiveness, and God's protection—or because it showed a spiritual dependence on God for that material need. But that's exactly the point: it's possible to pray a spiritual prayer for a physical need.

In 1 Kings 17, the prophet Elijah was staying with a widow in Zarephath when her son died. Elijah took the child, laid him on his own bed and prayed, "O LORD my God, let this child's life come into him again" (verse 21). Elijah asked God to give physical life back to the corpse that was lying right in front of him. This prayer is commended to us in the Bible, as part of Elijah's story, a story that demonstrated, over and over again, how connected Elijah was to God and his power. That connection included praying for the physical healing of a dead boy.

Now consider the case of the blind beggar Jesus healed along the road to Jericho:

> And they came to Jericho. And as he was leaving Jericho with his disciples and a great crowd, Bartimaeus, a blind beggar, the son of Timaeus, was sitting by the roadside. And when he heard that it was Jesus of Nazareth, he began to cry out and say, "Jesus, Son of David, have mercy on me!" And many rebuked him, telling him to be silent. But he cried out all the more, "Son of David, have mercy on me!" And Jesus stopped and said, "Call him." And they called the blind man, saying to him, "Take heart. Get up; he is calling you." And throwing off his cloak, he sprang up and came to Jesus. And Jesus said to him, "What do you want me to do for you?" And the blind man said to him, "Rabbi, let me recover my sight." And Jesus said to him, "Go your way; your faith has made you well." And immediately he recovered his sight and followed him on the way (Mark 10:46-52).

As Jesus walked by this poor man, Bartimaeus called out to him, using a spiritual-sounding expression: "Have mercy on me!" But, when Jesus asked him what he wanted, it turned out that the mercy he wanted was a physical blessing: "Rabbi, let me recover my sight" (v. 51). He didn't dress up his request with fancy words or by tying it to Jesus's

The Definition of Deep Prayer

ministry. He didn't say, "Jesus, I want to be one of the great signs to the people of Israel that you are the Messiah sent to save us, so please heal my blindness." He simply told Jesus what he wanted. Wherever we end up drawing the line between the deep and the shallow, it has to explain how a prayer for material blessing that meets a physical need can be deep.

A Definition of Deep Prayer

All these lines I drew between deep and shallow prayers, between good and bad prayers, between acceptable and unacceptable prayers, turned out to be lines the Bible doesn't draw. Each of these examples has shown us that a deep prayer may be answered by God or go unanswered; a deep prayer may focus on other people or on ourselves; a deep prayer may rise in praise or wallow in lament; a deep prayer may sing with eloquence or cry out in groans; a deep prayer may seek high and spiritual blessings or focus on the most basic of material needs. Our definition of deep prayer, therefore, has to account for all these biblical examples by drawing the line between the deep and the shallow in a place that accounts for these very different kinds of prayers being in the deep end. Our definition cannot just identify as deep an eloquent prayer of praise seeking a spiritual blessing for others that God wonderfully answers. It also has to account for a groaning prayer of lament about your own physical needs that God doesn't answer. If the definition of deep prayer can account for both of those kinds of prayers, then all these other lines will fade away and all that will matter is that we pray deeply.

Here is my definition of deep prayer: In deep prayer, you open yourself up to God, honestly and sincerely, approaching him as a person, talking to him in a way that deepens the relationship you have with him. The primary aim of deep prayer is deepening your relationship with God by openly and honestly talking to him about anything that's in your soul: your deepest feelings, thoughts, attitudes, and secrets; your true passions, goals, dreams, and pursuits; your joys, hardships, gratitude, and frustrations. When you pray deeply, you share yourself with God, person to person[5], in a growing and deepening relationship of love, trust, gratitude, and respect. An open and honest prayer for an intimately personal need is deeper than an eloquent, but impersonal,

---

[5]Throughout this book, I will be emphasizing the personhood of God. I believe that human personhood is derived from the personhood of God, that what we know as personal is a shadow of the personal God. If it's hard for you to think in those terms, John Frame may help: "Scripture rarely if ever uses the word *person* to describe God, or even to refer to the Father, the Son, or the Holy Spirit. But, like *Trinity*, *person* is an extrabiblical word that is very nearly unavoidable for us. It is the word in our vocabulary that applies to beings who speak, act intentionally, and so on. The biblical term *living* reinforces this picture. God is the living God, over against all the nonliving gods of the nations. Oaths in Scripture frequently begin with 'as surely as the Lord lives'" (Bible citations omitted). John M. Frame, *The Doctrine of God* (Phillipsburg, NJ: P&R Publishing, 2002) 27-28 (emphasis in original).

The Definition of Deep Prayer

prayer for national revival. A deep prayer isn't about the answer we get or who we pray for or the kinds of needs we present. It's about how personal, relational, and authentic the prayer is.

David's Deep Prayer (Psalm 51)

I mentioned earlier King David's prayer for the child he had with Bathsheba. David prayed that his child would live, even though God had told him the child would die. I wrote that I know David's prayers for the child's life were deep because part of what he prayed is recorded in Psalm 51. Now I can explain that the prayer recorded there is deep because it's open, vulnerable, and relational at its core.

Here is part of David's deep prayer:

> Have mercy on me, O God,
>   according to your steadfast love;
>   according to your abundant mercy
>   blot out my transgressions.
> Wash me thoroughly from my iniquity,
>   and cleanse me from my sin!
>
> For I know my transgressions,
>   and my sin is ever before me.
> Against you, you only, have I sinned
>   and done what is evil in your sight,
>   so that you may be justified in your words
>   and blameless in your judgment.
> Behold, I was brought forth in iniquity,
>   and in sin did my mother conceive me.
> Behold, you delight in truth in the inward being,

and you teach me wisdom in the secret heart.
Purge me with hyssop, and I shall be clean;
    wash me, and I shall be whiter than snow.
Let me hear joy and gladness;
    let the bones that you have broken rejoice.
Hide your face from my sins,
    and blot out all my iniquities.
Create in me a clean heart, O God,
    and renew a right spirit within me.
Cast me not away from your presence,
    and take not your Holy Spirit from me.
Restore to me the joy of your salvation,
    and uphold me with a willing spirit
    (vv. 1-12).

In the first lines of his prayer, David cried out to God using three deeply relational phrases: mercy (or unmerited favor), steadfast love, and abundant mercy (or compassion). We know that David was praying for God to spare the life of his child because, when David learned the child was dead, he stopped praying (2 Samuel 12:19-20). But David didn't pray an impersonal prayer, merely asking God to swoop down and save the baby's life. He was seeking a restoration of the relationship with God that his great sins had broken. David knew that his sin had put the child's life in danger, so he prayed a relational prayer, seeking God himself, openly confessing his sins, seeking God's forgiveness for his sins, all while longing for God's presence in his life. In this plea for restoration, inside a deepening relationship with God, David also asked God to spare his son's life. By pursuing a

The Definition of Deep Prayer

deeper relationship with God, David prayed a deep prayer for the child's physical health. What made it deep was David's openness and honesty as he pursued God as his Father and friend.

Biblical Warnings Against Impersonal Prayers

Back when I was drawing all those lines between good and bad prayers, I had to abandon every distinction I had made because the Bible commends prayers on both sides of all my lines. But now I know that I have finally discovered what makes a prayer deep because the Bible never commends impersonal, detached, ritualistic prayers. Instead, the Bible warns us against praying those kinds of prayers.

In the examples I use below, God speaks to unfaithful people of the old covenant who had rejected a relationship with him but still wanted to receive the benefits of the covenant God had made with Israel. The language here is strong, as God condemns their actions and judges the people. He is not talking to faithful Christians who are seeking God but haven't learned how to pray deep prayers regularly and intentionally. I wrote earlier that, as soon as you became a Christian, God started pulling you into deeper prayers with him. Now we know what that means: God started drawing you into a deeper relationship with him and, by doing that, has helped you to pray personal, relational prayers. There is no condemnation in these warnings for the praying Christian. I'm using these examples, however, because they show God's contempt at prayers (and other religious acts) that are performed without pursuing a relationship with him. The point is that, since this is God's view of non-relational religion, you will not be able to find a non-relational prayer commended in the Bible. And, as I said, that shows we have found the right line between the deep and the shallow.

First Warning: Forgetting What Sacrifices Are For

Psalm 50 records God's strong rebuke to people who brought animal sacrifices to the temple without understanding what those sacrifices were for:

> Hear, O my people, and I will speak;
> > O Israel, I will testify against you.
> > I am God, your God.
> Not for your sacrifices do I rebuke you;
> > your burnt offerings are continually before me.
> I will not accept a bull from your house
> > or goats from your folds.
> For every beast of the forest is mine,
> > the cattle on a thousand hills.
> I know all the birds of the hills,
> > and all that moves in the field is mine.
>
> If I were hungry, I would not tell you,
> > for the world and its fullness are mine.
> Do I eat the flesh of bulls
> > or drink the blood of goats?
> Offer to God a sacrifice of thanksgiving,
> > and perform your vows to the Most High,
> and call upon me in the day of trouble;

The Definition of Deep Prayer

I will deliver you, and you shall glorify me (vv. 7-15).

The first thing God wants them to know is that he is not rebuking them for failing to bring sacrifices to him—because they never failed to bring sacrifices to him: "Your burnt offerings are continually before me" (v. 8b). The problem was that they had forgotten the purpose behind the sacrifices. They seemed to think they were giving God bulls and goats and birds because God needed them, because God was weak and hungry and had to eat. This is a ridiculous view of God on a lot of levels but, "a superficial and formal offering of sacrifices, based on obedience to stipulations and nothing else was tantamount to such a [foolish] view of God."[6] What God rebuked was the bringing of sacrifices without seeking a relationship with him.

Second Warning: Following God While Rejecting God

The book of Isaiah is a long book that confronts the sins of a lot of different people—primarily the people of Israel and Judah, but also the many pagan nations across the world. These sins serve as the basis of both God's coming judgment and God's great salvation in Jesus Christ. In the very first chapter, Isaiah records God's anger at worship without relationship:

---

[6] Peter C. Craigie and Marvin E Tate, *Psalms 1-50*, 2 ed. *Word Biblical Commentary, v. 19* (Nashville, Thomas Nelson, Inc., 2004), 366.

DEEP PRAYER

> When you come to appear before me,
>   who has required of you
>   this trampling of my courts?
> Bring no more vain offerings;
>   incense is an abomination to me.
>   New moon and Sabbath and the calling of
>   convocations—
>   I cannot endure iniquity and solemn assembly.
> Your new moons and your appointed feasts
>   my soul hates;
>   they have become a burden to me;
>   I am weary of bearing them.
> When you spread out your hands,
>   I will hide my eyes from you;
>   even though you make many prayers,
>   I will not listen;
>   your hands are full of blood (Isaiah 1:12-15).

In this passage, God condemned the people for bringing animals into his temple, making offerings, and burning incense at every new moon and on every Sabbath day. Since God had commanded all of these, it cannot be the activities themselves that he condemned, but how they were being abused by the worshippers. God told them to stop bringing vain offerings to him (v. 13). "As used here, [vain] designates an offering or sacrifice, which from the formal and outward standpoint fulfilled the prescriptions of the Mosaic ritual, but which, *inasmuch as the heart that offered it was estranged from God*, was in reality nothing more than

The Definition of Deep Prayer

a dead work of hypocrisy."[7] God's attitude comes out in verse 13: "I cannot endure iniquity and solemn assembly," where the iniquity is their estrangement from God and their solemn assembly is their formal and outward ritual. The language here is strong, especially about prayer: "even though you make many prayers, I will not listen" (v. 15b).

Third Warning: A Den of Robbers

Jeremiah preached to the people of Judah at a different time from Isaiah, but he confronted a lot of the same sins. One of those sins was the belief that it was possible for the citizens of Judah to get blessings and forgiveness from God by following the rituals of the law and the temple, even when their hearts were far from God himself. At one point in his ministry, God told Jeremiah to stand in front of the great temple in Jerusalem and pronounce a powerful judgement:

> The word that came to Jeremiah from the LORD: "Stand in the gate of the LORD's house, and proclaim there this word, and say, Hear the word of the LORD, all you men of Judah who enter these gates to worship the LORD. Thus says the LORD of hosts, the God of Israel: Amend your ways and your deeds, and I will let you dwell in this place. Do not trust in these deceptive words: 'This is the temple of the LORD, the temple of the LORD, the temple of the LORD'" (Jeremiah 7:1-4).

---

[7] Edward J. Young, *The Book of Isaiah*, v. 1 (Grand Rapids, William B. Eerdmans Publishing Company, 1965), 65 (emphasis added).

DEEP PRAYER

These sinful people had assumed that, as long as they maintained the temple and its regular sacrifices, they would be safe from God's wrath against their sins. After all, they thought, the whole point of shedding all that blood in the temple was to cover over their sins.

They were wrong; not about the blood of the sacrifices covering sins, but by thinking this covering was an end in itself. God provided sacrifices that covered their sins so that they could know him, have a relationship with him, be his people. They completely missed the truth that God wasn't demanding ritual for ritual's sake, but for the sake of the relationship. Here is the rest of Jeremiah's message:

> Behold, you trust in deceptive words to no avail. Will you steal, murder, commit adultery, swear falsely, make offerings to Baal, and go after other gods that you have not known, and then come and stand before me in this house, which is called by my name, and say, "We are delivered!"—only to go on doing all these abominations? Has this house, which is called by my name, become a den of robbers in your eyes? Behold, I myself have seen it, declares the LORD (vv. 8-11).

A den of robbers is the place where robbers go after committing their robberies to be safe and hidden from the consequences of their crimes. These people were treating the temple of God like a den of robbers, thinking they could commit all the sins laid out in verses 8 and 9, run into the temple, receive forgiveness, and then go out again and commit more sins. This cavalier attitude about their sins

The Definition of Deep Prayer

showed they had no relationship with God, since they didn't care at all about the truth he had revealed, or about what he considers evil, or about what pleases him.

Fourth Warning: Jesus and the Pharisees

In one of the many confrontations Jesus had with the Pharisees and scribes, they asked him, "Why do your disciples break the tradition of the elders? For they do not wash their hands when they eat" (Matthew 15:1-2). These weren't public health experts concerned with the spreading of diseases. The handwashing they were concerned about wasn't for hygiene's sake but for ritualistic purity's sake. They believed that a person could not stand before God unless their traditions were followed.

Jesus answered them by showing how their traditions actually undermined the Word of God:

> He answered them, "And why do you break the commandment of God for the sake of your tradition? For God commanded, 'Honor your father and your mother,' and, 'Whoever reviles father or mother must surely die.' But you say, 'If anyone tells his father or his mother, "What you would have gained from me is given to God," he need not honor his father.' So for the sake of your tradition you have made void the word of God" (vv. 3-6).

That wasn't the real rebuke, however; that was just the prelude. Next, Jesus quoted Isaiah 29:13 to show them their hypocrisy: "You hypocrites! Well did Isaiah prophesy of you, when he said: 'This people honors me with their lips, *but their heart is far from me*; in vain do they worship me, teaching as doctrines the commandments of men'" (vv. 7-9).

Honoring God with lips only, without engaging your heart, is the very definition of a non-relational prayer, the shallow prayer that God hates.

Last Warning: To Praying Christians

The four warnings we have looked at have all been directed toward unbelievers, people who have abandoned God, who have no desire to know God, who hide their souls from God, but who also want to maintain the trappings of a biblical religion. These rebukes were not written to the sincere Christian seeking God through prayer. This last warning, however, is directed at Christians.

James wrote his letter to Jewish-Christian congregations scattered around the Roman Empire (James 1:1). In chapter four, he dealt with the problem of unanswered prayer and told them, "You ask and do not receive, because you ask wrongly, to spend it on your passions" (v. 3). For a long time, I assumed this verse meant that you cannot expect God to answer a prayer that asks him for things you can use to fulfill your sinful desires. While that's certainly true, it's not what James is warning against here. The prayer James is warning against is one that asks nothing from God but the thing being prayed for—a prayer that seeks the gift without much, or

The Definition of Deep Prayer

any, real thought of the giver.[8] God is offering himself to us, a real relationship with him through prayer, and the Christians James wrote to were ignoring the relationship and asking God to just give them the stuff they needed. That kind of prayer doesn't get answered because God rejects shallow prayers.

Responding to the Warnings

Reading all these warnings like this, one after another, may feel dark and negative (which it should for the person who doesn't have a relationship with God). And yes, God reveals sin in his Word, and those sins will condemn those who reject him. However, for Christians, God reveals our sin to push us toward what is good, even what is best for us in our lives. For example, God's commandment, "You shall not commit adultery" prohibits sexual promiscuity because this kind of unfaithfulness destroys lives and even mirrors humanity's sinful pursuit of other gods. But for the Christian, this prohibition reveals to us the beauty of marriage, and how its union is much greater, more fulfilling, more wonderful than any other relationship on earth. When God prohibits adultery, he also promotes marriage.

---

[8]*See*, Douglas J. Moo, *The Letter of James*, *The Pillar New Testament Commentary* (Grand Rapids, William B. Eerdmans Publishing Company, 2000), 185.

It's the same with these warnings and commandments against rituals performed for the sake of the ritual. Asking God to simply meet your needs, like he is some kind of impersonal power you can plug into, is a terrible sin. But all these prohibitions can also serve to promote a deeper, more wonderful relationship with God than mere ritual can provide. These warnings are God's declaration that he created all these things—the temple, the bloody sacrifices, and prayer—as a means of knowing and loving him. That's why the Bible never holds up as an example any prayer that fails to pursue a relationship with God; that's why the deepest prayers are not the most eloquent or the most spiritual, but the ones that pursue God himself.

Now that we have identified what makes a prayer deep, it's time to learn how to pray deep prayers regularly and intentionally. In chapter 2, we will see why Jesus's prayer in the Garden of Gethsemane is the deepest prayer recorded in the Bible. Then, in chapter 3, we will learn why we can use both Jesus's prayer and Jesus's relationship with his Father as a model for both our prayers and our own relationship with the Triune God. Once that foundation is laid, we will learn the language of deep prayer (chapter 4), how God uses deep prayer to pull us into a deeper relationship with him (chapter 5), and how that relationship deepens when we listen to God's side of the conversation (chapter 6). Finally, in chapter 7, we will learn the end of deep prayer by seeing

The Definition of Deep Prayer

what God's ultimate goal is for calling us to pray. My own prayer is that, by the end of the book, you will not only be praying deep prayers to God regularly and intentionally, but you will also experience the deep blessing of being in an intimate relationship with God.

CHAPTER 2

THE MODEL OF DEEP PRAYER

Deep prayers are relational prayers. When you pray deep prayers, you, as a person, talk to another person—to your Father in heaven, to Jesus your Savior, to the Holy Spirit dwelling inside you. When you pray deep prayers, you don't merely inform God of your needs and desires, you share your soul with him; you don't seek God as merely the power that can help you, but as a person you can know—and who you want to know—deeply and intimately. You can pray a deep prayer on your first day as a Christian while, twenty, thirty, or forty years later, your greater knowledge of God, your growing openness toward him, your deeper connection with him, your clearer understanding of yourself, will make your prayers—and your relationship—deeper, stronger, and more intimate.

If this is true of us, that with each passing decade our relationship with Father, Son, and Spirt grows deeper and deeper, then what does this say about Jesus? While Jesus walked on this earth, he was both fully human and fully God. That means, before he uttered his first prayer as a human being, he had spent an eternity in a relationship of

The Model of Deep Prayer

unimaginable intimacy with his Father in heaven. The doctrine of the Trinity teaches us that God exists as three distinct persons, all of whom share one divine nature and who, as spiritual beings, mutually indwell one another in a relationship impossible among humans: a relationship of perfection with perfection, of infinite depth of personality with infinite depth of personality; a connection of minds complete in knowledge, of hearts filled with love, of wills governed by holy wisdom. Jesus, by his very nature as God, lived in this eternal fellowship that satisfied every need. Try to imagine the love shared in this relationship: a love poured out eternally between Father, Son, and Spirit, a perfect love for the perfection of each person, a love that runs deep and cherishes each person infinitely, a love that's untarnished by any selfishness or hidden agenda or neediness or insecurity. When God tells us, in the Bible, that he is love (1 John 4:8, 16), this is what he is pointing to—his nature as a relationship in which love dominates. Love is an attribute of God's because relationship sits at the very core of God's nature.

Since that's the relationship Jesus had with his Father while up in heaven, then every prayer Jesus prayed to his Father while he was on earth was deeper than any prayer anyone else has ever prayed. The infinite depth of the relationships among the Trinity made every prayer he ever prayed on earth far deeper than we can comprehend. When Jesus stood before a crowd of hungry people with only five loaves of bread and two fish and "said a blessing" (Matthew 14:19), that was a far deeper prayer than anything I have ever prayed.

Just because every prayer of Jesus's was deeper than any prayer we have ever prayed doesn't mean that all the prayers of Jesus are equally deep, that one prayer could not be deeper than all the others. I believe that the prayer Jesus prayed in the Garden of Gethsemane was his deepest prayer. I believe that this conversation with his Father was vastly different from any he had before—both on earth and in heaven. Take a walk with me through that garden to see what I mean.

As Matthew 26 opens, the story is clearly turning to the upcoming death of Jesus. In the first two verses, Jesus told his disciples what was about to happen: "When Jesus had finished all these sayings, he said to his disciples, 'You know that after two days the Passover is coming, and the Son of man will be delivered up to be crucified'" (Matthew 26:1-2). Then, in verses 3 through 5, Matthew peeks into the palace of the high priest, where the elders of Israel gathered to talk about Jesus and, more specifically, how to get rid of this troublesome rabble-rouser in a way that wouldn't come back to bite them. In verses 6 through 13, we read about an unnamed woman who poured an entire flask of "very expensive ointment" on Jesus's head, a rash action that the

The Model of Deep Prayer

disciples called a huge waste of resources, but Jesus called "a beautiful thing" that was done "to prepare me for burial." Verses 14 through 16 record that Judas went to the chief priests to offer his services as a traitor—for a price, of course. Then, starting in verse 17, Matthew recounted the Passover meal Jesus ate with his disciples, the meal we call the Last Supper because we know that the crucifixion of Jesus is right around the corner. That's five rapid scenes all related to Jesus's coming death.

But, immediately after the Last Supper and just before the ordeal of the crucifixion, Jesus led his disciples out to the Garden of Gethsemane and prayed:

> Then Jesus went with them to a place called Gethsemane, and he said to his disciples, "Sit here, while I go over there and pray." And taking with him Peter and the two sons of Zebedee, he began to be sorrowful and troubled. Then he said to them, "My soul is very sorrowful, even to death; remain here, and watch with me." And going a little farther he fell on his face and prayed, saying, "My Father, if it be possible, let this cup pass from me; nevertheless, not as I will, but as you will." And he came to the disciples and found them sleeping. And he said to Peter, "So, could you not watch with me one hour? Watch and pray that you may not enter into temptation. The spirit indeed is willing, but the flesh is weak." Again, for the second time, he went away and prayed, "My Father, if this cannot pass unless I drink it, your will be done." And again he came and found them sleeping, for their eyes were heavy. So, leaving

them again, he went away and prayed for the third time, saying the same words again. Then he came to the disciples and said to them, "Sleep and take your rest later on. See, the hour is at hand, and the Son of Man is betrayed into the hands of sinners. Rise, let us be going; see, my betrayer is at hand" (Matthew 26:36-46).

At the very end of this long session of prayer, Jesus looked up and saw Judas leading a mob of Jews who were coming to arrest him. A few hours later, Jesus would be nailed to a cross by the Romans, gasping for every painful breath until he died. But, in those couple of hours between the end of the supper and his arrest by the mob, Jesus separated himself from his disciples because he desperately needed to be alone with his Father.

As the full weight of what he was about to do crashed down on Jesus, he cried out in pain to his Father, asking him to let him avoid going to the cross: "My Father, if it be possible, let this cup pass from me" (Matthew 26:39).

Now, to be fair, he didn't ask his Father to abandon the plan of salvation and just let all the sinners in the world die and go to hell. He asked the Father to find another way to save them: "*If it be possible,* let this cup pass from me." Let's skip the cross if there is some other way to accomplish this plan of salvation.

Where Did *That* Come From?

That's a shocking prayer. It's shocking because there isn't a single word in all the gospels that prepares us for this

The Model of Deep Prayer

prayer. Everything presented to us in all four gospels—every scene, every story, every confrontation, every parable, every instruction—shows Jesus as the willing Savior, marching straight to a crucifixion he knew was in his future. Just in the book of Matthew (never mind the other three gospel writers), Jesus told his disciples over and over about his coming death. Jesus wasn't surprised by the combination of circumstances that ended at the cross, he knew exactly where his actions were leading him, and he headed straight for it. Below are four passages from Matthew where Jesus talked to his disciples about his coming death. All four show that Jesus knew the cross was in his future, but the last two also show that Jesus was resolved to follow the Father's plan all the way to his death.

1. Matthew 16:21. Immediately after Peter's great confession that Jesus is the Christ, Jesus told his disciples clearly what was going to happen to him: "From that time Jesus began to show his disciples that he must go to Jerusalem and suffer many things from the elders and chief priests and scribes, and be killed, and on the third day be raised." Did you notice that little word "must"? He *must* go to Jerusalem. Not he might swing by Jerusalem; not it's one of the possibilities for his itinerary; but it was necessary and inevitable. He must go. He must suffer. He must be killed. He must be raised.

2. Matthew 17:22. When Jesus came down the mountain after the transfiguration, he revealed the plan to his disciples again: "As they were gathering in Galilee, Jesus said to them, 'The Son of Man is about to be delivered into the hands of men, and they will kill him, and he will be raised on the third day.' And they were greatly distressed." He again spoke of inevitable events settled in the mind of God, not of possibilities dependent on which way the political winds happened to blow, and not of contingencies, like he had an escape hatch ready and might be able to use it. He said, "The Son of Man is about to be delivered into the hands of men, and they *will* kill him."

3. Matthew 20:25-28. About a week before the Supper, Jesus not only reminded his disciples again about his death, but he also revealed that his death would be the culmination of Jesus's ministry on this earth and be the defining principle that would shape both his disciples' future ministry and the life of the church that would be created by his death:

> But Jesus called them to him and said, "You know that the rulers of the Gentiles lord it over them, and their great ones exercise authority over them. It shall not be so among you. But whoever would be great among you must be your servant, and whoever would be first among you must be your slave, even as the Son of Man came not to be served but to serve, *and to give his life as a ransom for many.*"

When the holy Son of God was hanging from the cross as a ransom for vile sinners, his disciples would see the ultimate example of service to others that they would need carry into their future ministry of preaching the gospel to the

The Model of Deep Prayer

nations around the world. Jesus could never run from the cross because he came to earth as the God who serves; because he was, in Isaiah's prophecy, the suffering servant; because the future church would need to be like Jesus, a body of people who serve one another.

4. Back to Matthew 16. Jesus also showed how fully he was committed to dying on the cross by his reaction when the plan was challenged by Peter following his first prediction in Matthew 16: "And Peter took him aside and began to rebuke him, saying, 'Far be it from you, Lord! This shall never happen to you'" (Matthew 16:22). Remember, Peter had just confessed that Jesus is the Christ, the Son of the living God, and Jesus had told Peter that God himself had revealed this to him, that he was the rock on which Jesus would build a church that even the gates of hell would not be able assail, and that he would give Peter the keys to the kingdom. After hearing all that, maybe Peter thought he now had permission to give Jesus his thoughts about his plans and his mission. Or maybe he was just shocked that the world's most horrible torture could happen to Jesus. Or maybe he just thought that it was impossible that the man, who he had just declared to be God, could ever die. Whatever Peter's reasons for speaking up, Jesus showed him how wrong he was, calling Peter's thinking Satanic and opposed to the very purposes of God: "Get behind me, Satan! You are a hindrance to me. For you are not setting your mind on the things of God, but on the things of man" (Matthew 16:23).

DEEP PRAYER

The Prayer We Were Expecting

If you were reading this gospel for the first time and had no knowledge of the rest of the story, what kind of prayer would you expect Jesus to pray on the night he was betrayed and arrested? We have heard the story of Gethsemane so often, it's hard to detach ourselves from the grief-stricken prayer Jesus actually prayed in that garden that night. But try to imagine what your expectations would be if you read Jesus's repeated and powerful commitments to his mission without knowing the rest of the story.

I think we would expect Jesus to pray for the success of that mission: achieving its goals in the next couple of days, protecting his chosen disciples from the evil that was coming, sending those disciples out into a hostile world to proclaim the message of the gospel, and the spreading of this message to others around the world and across time. That kind of a prayer would make perfect sense in the flow of the story.

Well, as it turns out, Jesus prayed that exact prayer at the end of the Last Supper, before leading his disciples into the garden that night. Matthew didn't record that prayer for us, but John did. The prayer John records in chapter 17 is the prayer we expected to hear:

> When Jesus had spoken these words, he lifted up his eyes to heaven, and said, "Father, the hour has come; glorify your Son that the Son may glorify you, since you have given him authority over all flesh, to give eternal

The Model of Deep Prayer

life to all whom you have given him. And this is eternal life, that they know you the only true God and Jesus Christ whom you have sent. I glorified you on earth, having accomplished the work that you gave me to do. And now, Father, glorify me in your own presence with the glory that I had with you before the world existed" (John 17:1-5).

In this prayer, Jesus's bloody and painful death on the cross is described as the Father glorifying the Son so that the Son may glorify the Father. Jesus is clear on his mission: to give eternal life to the people the Father had given to him. Without a hint of grief or pain or hesitation, Jesus prays as though his work is already completed and he is just waiting for the Father to give him back the glory he used to have with him in heaven.

Then he prayed for his disciples, recalling his ministry among them, their place in the Father's plan, and their positive and growing relationship with Jesus:

> I have manifested your name to the people whom you gave me out of the world. Yours they were, and you gave them to me, and they have kept your word. Now they know that everything that you have given me is from you. For I have given them the words that you gave me, and they have received them and have come to know in truth that I came from you; and they have believed that you sent me. I am praying for them. I am not praying for the world but for those whom you have given me, for they are yours (John 17:6-9).

He went on to pray that these men would be protected as

they go out into a hostile world: "Holy Father, keep them in your name" (verse 11) and "I do not ask that you take them out of the world, but that you keep them from the evil one" (verse 15). Then he sent them out into the world with the message of the gospel: "As you sent me into the world, so I have sent them into the world" (verse 18). After praying for the eleven eating with him at that table, he turned his attention to the spreading of the gospel all over the world and across the centuries:

> I do not ask for these only, but also for those who will believe in me through their word, that they may all be one, just as you, Father, are in me, and I in you, that they also may be in us, so that the world may believe that you have sent me. The glory that you have given me I have given to them, that they may be one even as we are one, I in them and you in me, that they may become perfectly one, so that the world may know that you sent me and loved them even as you loved me. Father, I desire that they also, whom you have given me, may be with me where I am, to see my glory that you have given me because you loved me before the foundation of the world (vv. 20-24).

This is the mission-focused prayer by a mission-focused Jesus that we have been led to expect just before Jesus willingly gave his life to bring his people to glory and give them eternal life.

But then, after leaving the supper and walking into the garden, this steadfast march to the cross was interrupted when Jesus asked his Father in heaven to find another way.

The Model of Deep Prayer

The Pain in the Prayer

If Jesus knew his mission, if he repeatedly endorsed the mission, if he worked so hard to fulfill the mission, and if he prayed for the success of the mission, then how could he, right before the climax of the mission, ask the Father to change the mission?

Matthew gave us the answer in verse 37 of chapter 26: "And taking with him Peter and the two sons of Zebedee, he began to be sorrowful and troubled." How did Matthew know what Jesus was feeling at that specific moment? Because Jesus told Peter, James, and John exactly how he felt: "Then he said to them, 'My soul is very sorrowful, even to death; remain here, and watch with me'" (v. 38).

Jesus prayed this shocking prayer because he was in deep pain and, expressing his deep pain, he asked his Father to let him avoid the cross. But why was he in such deep pain? What could have caused a pain so deep that Jesus could ask the Father to throw off a plan that was literally an eternity in the making?

One theory is that Jesus simply got scared as he was facing the prospect of a painful death. After all, you can plan all you want, but when it comes time to execute the plan, when things move from theory to reality, you can always have second thoughts.

I think that's wrong. For one thing, the idea of Jesus lacking physical courage is laughable. After he willingly surrendered his exalted, spiritual position in heaven to become a baby in a stable, after he endured the hardships of his ministry without a complaint, and after he overcame every kind of temptation thrown at him, it's not plausible that he would recoil from finishing his mission by shrinking in fear from the cross.

A second theory is that having the sins of the world imputed to him, and bearing the penalty for those sins, horrified the sinless, holy Jesus into praying to sidestep the cross. This view is plausible, but I have doubts about it. In Hebrews 12:2 we're told that, for the joy set before him, Jesus endured the cross and the shame that went along with it. In other words, Jesus could look past the ordeal of the cross and see the "great multitude that no one could number, from every nation, from all tribes and peoples and languages" that would be saved by his sacrifice (Revelation 7:9). Seeing that result filled Jesus with a joy that carried him through both the physical pain of dying on the cross and the spiritual turmoil of becoming sin after never knowing sin.

The Greatest Horror of the Cross

I have a different theory. I think that Jesus looked past the physical pain, past the imputation of human sin, and saw the most horrifying consequence of dying on the cross as a sacrifice for sins and a substitute for sinners. At the key moment of his crucifixion, the relationship between Jesus and his Father would, for the first time in his eternal

The Model of Deep Prayer

existence, be broken. While on the cross, Jesus wouldn't be connected to his Father.

Don't dismiss this as a small thing, like a husband going away on a business trip and missing his wife for a couple of nights. Up until that night, the very core of Jesus's existence was the relationships he had with the Father and the Holy Spirit. These relationships define who Jesus is; these relationships had existed in intimate joy for all eternity; these relationships are rooted in Jesus's nature as God himself; and these relationships had been unbreakable until Jesus, by hanging on the cross to save sinners, broke them. No matter how much joy was set before Jesus, no matter how much good was accomplished by the cross, no matter how much glory would shine on the Father, there would always be a time when the Father and the Son weren't intimately connected to each other.

Was this impending separation between Father and Son really such a big deal? Yes, it was, and the Bible tells us how big a deal it was in a prophecy made centuries before Jesus died on the cross—actually, centuries before the horrible torture that is crucifixion was even invented. In Psalm 22, the Holy Spirit inspired David to describe the crucifixion vividly, using phrases like, "all my bones are out of joint" and "my heart is like wax, it is melted within my breast" (v. 14), and "they have pierced my hands and feet" (v. 16), and even, "they divide my garments among them, and for my clothing they cast lots" (v. 18). That's an amazingly detailed prophecy describing crucifixion in general and Jesus's death in particular.

But do you remember how Psalm 22 starts? David cried out, "My God, my God, why have you forsaken me?" In this prophecy about the death of Jesus on the cross, the Holy Spirit revealed to David that the foremost thing on Jesus's mind would be his separation from his Father. Then, centuries later, on that hill just outside of Jerusalem, the Holy Spirit confirmed this by inspiring Matthew, as he wrote his gospel, to record only one thing Jesus said while hanging on the cross: "'*Eli, Eli, lema sabachthani*?' that is, 'My God, my God, why have you forsaken me?'" (Matthew 27:46). When Jesus hung on that cross, he lamented his separation from the Father, just as David had prophesied, a separation Jesus saw coming while he prayed in Gethsemane, and which caused him such intense pain and grief that he asked his Father to find another way. That's what makes this Jesus's deepest prayer. Yes, he had his eternal, spiritual, intimate relationship with the Father that made all his prayers deep but, in that garden, he wasn't just praying inside his relationship with the Father, he was praying *about* his relationship with the Father—even *for* his relationship with the Father.

Using Gethsemane as a Model Prayer

But can Jesus's prayer in the garden really be a model for our prayers? So much of what went on in that garden was

The Model of Deep Prayer

unique to Jesus. He was praying about a unique, unrepeatable event in world history. And he was praying as a unique being—as God in human flesh. When we consider the uniqueness of the event and just how different we are from Jesus, we could easily conclude that the way Jesus talked to his Father cannot possibly be a model for our prayers. Instead, Gethsemane may seem more like holy ground, something we observe but cannot participate in.

But Jesus's prayers in that garden could still be a model for our prayers if our relationship with God is somehow analogous to Jesus's relationship with his Father. So, instead of asking how our relationship with God is different from Jesus's relationship with his Father, we need to ask if there is some way in which our relationship with God can be like Jesus's relationship with his Father. If there are ways our relationships are similar, then what we saw and heard in Gethsemane can be a model, and we need to learn whatever we can from Jesus's prayer, we need to follow his example as best we can, and we need to pursue the deepest relationship with God that is possible for us.

Fortunately, we don't have to speculate on whether human sinners can have a relationship with the holy God or, if they can, what kind of relationship we could have. God himself has defined in the Bible exactly what kind of relationship he pursues with us. In the next chapter, we will listen to God's definition and find out just how fully, how completely, how intimately God gives himself to his relationship with us. This is the relationship of deep prayer that we pursue every time we talk to God.

CHAPTER 3

THE RELATIONSHIP OF DEEP PRAYER

The courtroom drama has been a staple of literature, plays, movies, and television for as long as we have had books, theaters, cinemas, and TV sets, ranging from the socially serious *To Kill a Mockingbird*[9] to the culturally irreverent *My Cousin Vinny*[10], to the screwball silliness of *What's Up Doc?*[11] and everything in between. Courtroom scenes play on themes of both justice and injustice, whether it's the railroading of Edmond Dantes to protect the prosecutor's family,[12] or the work of Jake Brigance to win equal justice for his black client in the deep South,[13] or the

---

[9] Harper Lee, *To Kill a Mockingbird* (New York, First Perennial Classics, 2002).
[10] Jonathan Lynn (Director). 1992. *My Cousin Vinny* [Film]. 20th Century Fox.
[11] Peter Bogdonovich (Director). 1972. *What's Up Doc?* [Film]. Warner Brothers.
[12] Alexandre Dumas, *The Count of Monte Cristo* (New York, Penguin Books, 1849, 1996).
[13] John Grisham, *A Time to Kill* (New York: Island Books, 1989).

thief and corrupter of youth, Fagin, finally getting his just deserts.[14]

The gospel is truly the greatest courtroom drama ever told; it's the one, beautiful story embedded in our world—our souls, even—of which all other stories are but the echo.[15] Just put yourself in the drama of this story. Picture yourself being dragged into a courtroom through the prisoners' entrance dressed in an orange jumpsuit and wearing manacles on your wrists and ankles. You see walls paneled with rich, intimidating mahogany. You see the high and imposing judge's bench. Across the room, you see the prosecutor's table piled with boxes filled with evidence of your crimes and you see the devil himself sitting there, ready to accuse you. You're shoved into a seat at the defendant's table where you sit alone, without a lawyer. You know you're in trouble. You know you committed the sins standing against you. You even acknowledge (but only to yourself) that you *wanted* to commit them, that you *enjoyed*

---

[14]Charles Dickens, *Oliver Twist* (New York, Puffin Classics, 1837, 1994).

[15]"[T]he story of the Bible—the story of salvation history—really is the greatest story ever told. It's the story that interprets and measures all other stories. It's been told in perfect order, in 'the fullness of time' (Gal. 4:4; Eph. 1:10). It's a story that is both written into our DNA (Rom. 1:20) and impossible to believe apart from a miracle (1 Cor. 1:20–31). The world both longs to hear this story and hates its proclamation." Mike Cosper, *The Stories We Tell: How TV and Movies Long for and Echo the Truth* (Wheaton, IL: Crossway, 2014), 17, Apple Books.

committing them, and that you would do them all again if you could. The only defense you can come up with for all the evidence stacked against you is that you weren't as bad as you could have been and that you were better than a lot of others were.

However, as soon as the Judge shows up, your hopes are crushed. He is clearly a strict and exacting Judge who holds the law up as a standard of perfect justice. He only cares about one thing: whether you have ever, even once, violated his precious law. He doesn't care if others have broken more laws than you, only if you have ever broken the law. He doesn't care about the times you succeeded in keeping the law, only about the times you failed. At that moment, you know your case is lost, that the verdict will be guilty, and the punishment will be severe.

Every person born on this earth starts off life in this terrifying situation. We may try to deny it or ignore it or explain it away or pretend everything is fine, but this is reality. And notice that, in this reality, the only relationship possible with God is one of a guilty criminal with a righteous judge. But, of course, that's not the whole story (at least for Christians). At the very moment the Judge has raised his gavel, poised to pound it on his bench and render the guilty verdict, someone bursts through the doors in the back of the courtroom, approaches the bench and calls himself your Advocate. He tells the Judge that you have put your faith and trust in him, that he has paid the penalty for all your sins himself, and that it would be unjust for the Judge to exact another penalty on you for those same crimes. Therefore, he says, you should be set free. Now everything has changed. You're not alone; you have a defense; you have a substitute who has made the ultimate sacrifice. Your Advocate then pleads for a verdict consistent with perfect justice. But then, in that moment, the Judge does something unexpected. Instead of switching his verdict from Guilty to Not Guilty, he hands down a verdict of Completely Exonerated in Jesus![16]

That's the gospel story, and it's every Christian's story. The sins may be different, and the events that led us into that courtroom are certainly different, but the drama plays out like that for all of us. And we rejoice in it all: the punishment that once terrified us has been borne by another; the sins that once defined us, weighed on us, and burdened us, have been paid in full; the justice that once condemned us now sets us

---

[16] Our legal system uses only the verdicts Guilty and Not Guilty, but the Not Guilty verdict in our system includes reasons that fall far below the Judge's verdict of exoneration, things like not guilty by reason of insanity or not guilty because of a technicality, or a verdict from a jury designed to protest an unjust law or a heavy-handed prosecutor (this is known as jury nullification). All these verdicts say the same thing: yes, he committed the crime, but he will not be punished for it. In the gospel, the verdict says something different: he is set free because he is deemed, in Jesus, to not even have committed the crime!

The Relationship of Deep Prayer

free. And—most importantly—our relationship with God has been transformed forever.

Unfortunately, many, many Christians, even after being set free, still see the Father as the righteous Judge ready to pounce on them with his unbending, exacting law. Some of those Christians actually expect the verdict freeing them to be reversed at some point in the future when they fall into another sin or—even worse—fall into the same, familiar sin a couple of hundred more times. Others think that it's only Jesus who loves them, not the Father and, apart from the infinite love and amazing grace of Jesus, the Father's wrath would be unleased upon them. But none of these thoughts is consistent with the gospel. Through the gospel, once a Christian hears the verdict of "Completely Exonerated in Jesus" he or she leaves the courtroom forever.

Forever and ever and ever.

Defining the Relationship

While we were standing in that courtroom, before Jesus came bursting in and changed everything, our relationship with God was defined as that of a guilty criminal before a righteous Judge. But Jesus transformed the very nature and character of our relationship with the Triune God. Now the question is, what kind of relationship do we have with God once we leave the courtroom?

Before we answer that question, we have to acknowledge that God alone has the authority to define his relationship with us; we do not have that right. We cannot get any closer to God than he allows us to, but we also shouldn't hold ourselves at a greater distance from God than he calls us to. This is simply his prerogative as God. If he wants to hold us at arm's length, then nothing we do will be able to get us closer to him. Likewise, if he calls us into an intimate relationship with him, it's not noble humility to play hard to get. Therefore, it's important that you know exactly how God defines his relationship with you and then, once his expectations are clear, it's essential that you pursue that kind of relationship with him.

That is what we're going to look at now, exactly how God—Father, Son, and Holy Spirit—defines his relationship with us after we have left the courtroom. As we make our way through the Bible's teaching, we're going to learn something amazing: God defines the relationship he pursues with us by comparing it to the most intimate relationships we can have as human beings. I'm going to do my best to describe this indescribable intimacy, but keep in mind that the intimacy, the beauty, the joy inside these relationships is far greater than I can convey in these few paragraphs. My goal isn't to describe the indescribable, it's to urge you to pursue this intimacy with God with all your heart, all your mind, and all your soul so you can experience it all for yourself.

The Relationship of Deep Prayer

The Father Adopts

When we survey the wonderous cross, I think it's natural to see, in the sacrifice of God himself, just how far God had to go to save our depraved and rebellious souls. But I think we should see more than that. While we contemplate the agony Jesus endured as he died on the cross, we should see just how far God was willing to go to have a relationship with us. I say that because Paul told the Galatians that God didn't send his Son to this earth merely to redeem people from their sin; he redeemed people from their sin so that they could become part of his family:

> But when the fullness of time had come, God sent forth his Son, born of woman, born under the law, to redeem those who were under the law, *so that* we might receive adoption as sons. And because you are sons, God has sent the Spirit of his Son into our hearts, crying, "Abba! Father!" So you are no longer a slave, but a son, and if a son, then an heir through God (Galatians 4:4-7).

Yes, the Incarnation was a pivotal event in human history. Of course, redemption is an enormous miracle in the life of every Christian. Yet, as important as both these are, Paul says they are not the ultimate act of God in Jesus Christ. Instead, they serve a higher purpose: "*so that* we might receive adoption as sons." Jesus's work secured a pardon for our sins, that's true; but the pardon was only the prelude to the real goal: our adoption by God the Father into his family. And this adoption isn't just a formality. Paul describes the relationship created in the adoption as full sonship. First, the Father sends his Spirit into our hearts to give us the freedom to speak to our new Father in intimate terms. Second, he lets us know that we're not just part of his household, like a slave might be, but that we are his sons. Third, as sons, we're given a full inheritance as part of his family. In his classic book, *Knowing God*, theologian J. I. Packer wrote that adoption is "the highest privilege that the gospel offers: higher even than justification . . . because of the richer relationship with God that it involves."[17]

Several years after writing to the Galatians, Paul wrote the same thing to the church at Rome:

> For all who are led by the Spirit of God are *sons of God*. For you did not receive the spirit of slavery to fall back into fear, but you have received the *Spirit of adoption as sons*, by whom we cry, "Abba! Father!" The Spirit himself bears witness with our spirit that we are *children of God*, and if children, then heirs—*heirs of God and fellow heirs with Christ*, provided we suffer with him in order that we may also be glorified with him (Romans 8:14-17).

The context is different, but the message is the same: Jesus didn't go to the cross, suffer through his separation with his Father, and die in agony to keep us in slavery under a new master. Jesus died so that we could become the

---

[17] J. I. Packer, *Knowing God* (Downers Grove, IL: InterVarsity Press, 1973, 1993), 206.

The Relationship of Deep Prayer

adopted children of God the Father and have an intimate relationship with him. In both these passages, the Spirit gives us permission to use the phrase, "Abba! Father!" when addressing God. "Abba" was a word Jesus himself used to speak to his Father while crying out to him in Gethsemane (Mark 14:36). The Spirit leads us to talk to our Father in heaven with the same intimacy as Jesus himself. In both these passages, Paul also mentions our inheritance—that as sons we also become heirs of God. But in this passage, Paul says that this inheritance is wrapped up in unimaginable glory.

God the Father defines the relationship he pursues with us not as a judge to a criminal or even as a benevolent master to a valued slave, but as a Father to a son. He compares his relationship with us to one of the most intimate relationships we can experience in our lives. The relationship we have with our parents shapes our view of the world, molds our earliest character, and sets, at the least, our first few steps into the world. I have known adults who are still so closely connected to their parents that this relationship still shapes and molds them. I have even known adult children of abusive parents who cannot break free of the harm inflicted on them by this relationship. That's how intimate, how important, this relationship is. For good or for evil, this relationship is embedded into the core of our souls.

DEEP PRAYER

God, of course, is the perfect Father. His perfection means we cannot carry the hurts, abuses, or abandonments of our own fathers into the definition of God's Fatherhood. As his children, we are made according to his own image (Gen 1:26-27). He is the Father who has compassion on his children (Psalm 103:13-14). He never leaves us or forsakes us (Hebrews 13:5). He graciously gives us all things (Romans 8:32), including everything we need for life and godliness (2 Peter 1:3). His love for us is deep and real (1 John 3:1-2) and can be seen as much in his discipline as in his blessings (Hebrews 12:7-11). Our Father leads us with infinite wisdom (Romans 11:33), and is molding our character to its highest virtue possible (Romans 8:29). So, as you embrace the Father's definition of his relationship with you, you not only have to acknowledge that he is your Father, but you also have to accept God as the greatest possible Father who seeks the most intimate relationship possible between a parent and child. If your experience as a child was marked by pain rather than blessing, by disappointment rather than encouragement, by rejection rather than faithfulness, or by indifference rather than love, you have to abandon your idea of the parent-child relationship and let God be the Father to you that you never had.

The Relationship of Deep Prayer

The Son Betroths

The only human relationship more intimate than the relationship between a parent and a child is the relationship between a husband and a wife. And so, God uses marriage as a metaphor for his relationship with his people all throughout the Bible.

It starts early. When God created the world—throwing stars and galaxies across the vastness of space and carefully crafting the intricate world of individual cells—he also created the first woman out of the rib of the first man and recorded the first marriage: "Therefore a man shall leave his father and his mother and hold fast to his wife, and they shall become one flesh. And the man and his wife were both naked and were not ashamed" (Genesis 2:24-25). This passage reveals to us that the deep intimacy shared by a husband and a wife was built into marriage right at its creation. First, the man shifts his priorities by leaving his father and mother so that he can devote himself to his wife with both passion and permanence. Next, the husband and wife become one in every way, physically, emotionally, and spiritually. Finally, before the Fall, their relationship is one of complete openness and honesty, so that they could stand before each other completely naked and feel no shame, no hesitation, no vulnerability, no self-consciousness.[18]

Then, with the marriage relationship created and defined by God, marriage became the foundational cultural institution of all people everywhere, even after the Fall, even after the Flood, even after the disruption caused by the tower at Babel. God created marriage and spread it all over the world so he could use marriage to define the relationship he intended to have with his people.

When God called Moses from out of a burning bush and commissioned him (over Moses's own objections) to lead Israel out of slavery in Egypt, he made a covenant promise to him that sounds like a proposal of marriage: "I will take you to be my people, and I will be your God" (Exodus 6:7). Centuries later, after Israel had been an unfaithful wife to God over and over again, God described the covenant he made with them as "the day when I took them by the hand to bring them out of the land of Egypt, my covenant that they broke, *though I was their husband*, declares the LORD" (Jeremiah 31:32). When God said this, he was announcing a new covenant, a covenant in which God will put his law inside his people, writing it not on tablets of stone, but on their very hearts. While the nature of the covenant is

---

[18]*See*, Gordon J. Wenham, *Genesis 1-15*, *Word Biblical Commentary*, vol. 1 (Waco, TX, Word, Inc., 1987), 70-72.

The Relationship of Deep Prayer

different, the promise is the same: "And I will be their God and they shall be my people" (Jeremiah 31:33).[19]

Throughout that history of covenant failure by the people of Israel, God would sometimes compare their idolatry—the chasing after other gods—with adultery—the chasing after other men.[20] This culminated in the book of Hosea, where God's prophet was directed to marry a woman known for her infidelity and who left Hosea to chase after other men. Of all the judgments in all the prophets, none is more devastating than when God declares to Israel, "you are not my people, and I am not your God" (Hosea 1:9).

Although God's marriage to Israel fell apart, God never abandoned his covenant to be God to his people. As Paul wrote, "Does [Israelite] unfaithfulness nullify the faithfulness of God? By no means! Let God be true though everyone were a liar" (Romans 3:3). Instead, God sent Jesus to be the mediator of a better covenant by presenting his church to himself as his bride.

In the New Testament, Jesus becomes the husband and the church becomes his bride. This image is used to describe the consummation of God's great victory over all evil in the

---

[19] *See, also*, Leviticus 26:12; Jeremiah 7:23, 11:4, 30:22; Ezekiel 36:28.
[20] In these passages, it's always the woman who is unfaithful, not because women have a greater propensity toward cheating, but because Israel was the unfaithful one in the relationship and is always depicted as the bride.

world when, in Revelation 19, the marriage supper of Jesus and his bride is celebrated:

> Then I heard what seemed to be the voice of a great multitude, like the roar of many waters and like the sound of mighty peals of thunder, crying out,
> "Hallelujah!
> For the Lord our God
>   the Almighty reigns.
> Let us rejoice and exult
>   and give him the glory,
>   for the marriage of the Lamb has come,
>   and his Bride has made herself ready;
> it was granted her to clothe herself
>   with fine linen, bright and pure"—
> for the fine linen is the righteous deeds of the saints (Revelation 19:6-8).

Although this marriage celebration takes place in heaven, the betrothal takes place here on the earth when a repentant sinner comes to Jesus. That's what Paul told the Christians in Corinth: "For I feel a divine jealousy for you, since I betrothed you to one husband, to present you as a pure virgin to Christ" (2 Corinthians 11:2).

Unfortunately, when sinners marry sinners in a fallen world,[21] the intimacy built into the relationship by God can lead to abuse, manipulation, brokenness. But just like with

---

[21] That's Paul David Tripp's pithy but insightful description of marriage in *What did you Expect? Redeeming the Realities of Marriage* (Wheaton, IL, Crossway, 2010).

The Relationship of Deep Prayer

the parent-child relationship, you cannot let your own experience of marriage define the marriage relationship Jesus pursues with you. To drive that point home, when Paul instructs Christian men on how to be good husbands, he does it by describing the kind of husband Jesus is, the kind of love Jesus pours on his bride inside this marriage.

> Husbands, love your wives, as Christ loved the church and gave himself up for her, that he might sanctify her, having cleansed her by the washing of water with the word, so that he might present the church to himself in splendor, without spot or wrinkle or any such thing, that she might be holy and without blemish. In the same way husbands should love their wives as their own bodies. He who loves his wife loves himself. For no one ever hated his own flesh, but nourishes and cherishes it, just as Christ does the church, because we are members of his body. "Therefore a man shall leave his father and mother and hold fast to his wife, and the two shall become one flesh." This mystery is profound, and I am saying that it refers to Christ and the church. However, let each one of you love his wife as himself, and let the wife see that she respects her husband (Ephesians 5:25-33).

The point of this passage is to tell husbands how to love their wives. But Paul's method is to show husbands how Jesus loves the church and then call on husbands to imitate Jesus. So, although your own personal experience of human marriage may not look like this passage, this passage is the description of your marriage with Jesus as part of the bride of Christ. If you're the wife of an abusive husband, or you're the husband of an unfaithful wife, those failures do not limit the intimacy and joy and blessing found in your marriage to Jesus. Your relationship with him should be marked by what marriage was created to be, a relationship of complete openness and honesty, where your fears, weaknesses, vulnerabilities, mistakes, and even sins can be exposed because you know they will all be covered in love and forgiveness. In marriage, this kind of relationship isn't created simply by saying, "I Do." However, we can grow our marriage into this because that's the nature of marriage. In the same way, this kind of relationship with Jesus isn't created by saying, "I Believe," but it can grow into this because that's the nature of our salvation and reconciliation.

The marriage metaphor describing our relationship with Jesus isn't exhausted by the few passages that refer to the church as the bride of Christ. Throughout the New Testament, everything we have as Christians is actually built on the foundation of Jesus as our husband and the church as his bride, even when those words are not used. Just as the hallmark of the marriage relationship is the union between a husband and his wife—"and the two will become one flesh"—so the hallmark of the Christian's relationship with Jesus is union with him. This teaching is so important and so extensive, that theologians have developed a doctrine around

The Relationship of Deep Prayer

it: the doctrine of Union with Christ.[22]

Marriage is the foundation of this doctrine because Union with Christ gathers up several different ways the New Testament describes the relationship we have with Jesus—that we are in Christ, that Christ is in us, that we are like Christ, and that we are with Christ[23]—all of which form a picture of the perfect marriage, where the husband and the wife are so intimately connected that they each begin to take on the best qualities of the other and their lives are defined by the time they spend with each other. The New Testament has way too much detail about what happens inside the soul of the Christian because we are united to Christ for me to try to present it here, but here is the verse that summarizes it all: "Blessed be the God and Father of our Lord Jesus Christ, who has blessed us *in Christ* with *every spiritual blessing* in the heavenly places" (Ephesians 1:3).

---

[22]Wayne Grudem, "Union with Christ," in *Systematic Theology: An Introduction to Biblical Doctrine* (Grand Rapids, Zondervan Publishing House, 1994), 840-850; Robert Letham, *Union with Christ: In Scripture, History, and Theology* (Phillipsburg, NJ, P&R Publishing, 2011); J. Todd Billings, *Union with Christ: Reframing Theology and Ministry for the Church* (Grand Rapids, Baker Academic, 2011); Rankin Wilbourne, *Union with Christ: The Way to Know and Enjoy God* (Colorado Springs, David C. Cook, 2016).

[23]"*Union with Christ is a phrase used to summarize several different relationships between believers and Christ, through which Christians receive every benefit of salvation. These relationships include the fact that we are in Christ, Christ is in us, we are like Christ, and we are with Christ.*" Grudem, 840 (italics in original).

DEEP PRAYER

There isn't a single spiritual blessing that you could think of that the Bible doesn't attribute to the marriage relationship—to our union—with Jesus.[24] This should shape how you pursue the blessings you need from God. Whether you need grace to get through hard circumstances or encouragement to stay faithful or freedom from sin or peace with the people around you, understand that God doesn't drop these into your life like Santa leaving presents under the tree. All of these blessings are given to us in Christ—as part of the relationship we have with Jesus. So, you can beg God for more grace, but that grace will come to you through a deeper relationship with your betrothed. Just as God warns us not to pray impersonal prayers, so God never gives us

---

[24]Here is a quick (and incomplete) tour through Paul's epistles. In Romans: redemption is in Christ Jesus (3:24); we are dead to sin and alive to God in Christ Jesus (6:11); we have eternal life in Christ Jesus our Lord (6:23); the Spirit has set us free in Christ Jesus (8:2); the love of God is in Christ Jesus our Lord (8:38-39). In 1 Corinthians: the church is sanctified in Christ Jesus (1:2); God's grace is given in Christ Jesus (1:4). In 2 Corinthians: God leads us in triumphal procession in Christ (2:14); anyone in Christ is a new creation (5:17); God is reconciling the world to himself in Christ (5:18-19). In Galatians: we have freedom in Christ (2:4); we are justified through faith in Christ (2:16); in Christ Jesus we are sons of God (3:26). In Ephesians: we hope in Christ (1:12); grace and kindness are shown to us in Christ Jesus (2:7); he himself is our peace (2:14); God forgave us in Christ (4:32). In Philippians: we have encouragement in Christ (2:1); the mindset of humility is ours in Christ Jesus (2:5-6); our righteousness is in Christ (3:9); the peace of God guards our hearts and minds in Christ Jesus (4:7); In Colossians: we are becoming mature in Christ (1:28); our faith is in Christ (2:5). In 1 Timothy: grace and love are in Christ Jesus (1:14).

impersonal blessings. Every blessing we receive from God is the fruit of our marriage relationship with Jesus.

The Spirit Indwells

Marriage may be the most intimate relationship human beings can have on this earth, but there is one relationship—not among humans and not on this earth—that's even more intimate. It's the eternal, spiritual, mutually indwelling relationships inside the Trinity itself. The Father, the Son, and the Holy Spirit all share the same divine nature by mutually indwelling one another so fully and so completely that, while there are three divine persons in the Trinity, there is only one God.

We only know this because Jesus explained it to his 11 remaining disciples during the Last Supper. He started by declaring to them, "If you had known me, you would have known my Father also. From now on you do know him and have seen him" (John 14:7). This prompted Philip to say, "Lord, show us the Father, and it is enough for us" (verse 8). Here is Jesus's response:

> Have I been with you so long, and you still do not know me, Philip? Whoever has seen me has seen the Father. How can you say, 'Show us the Father'? Do you not believe that *I am in the Father and the Father is in me*? The words that I say to you I do not speak on my own authority, but *the Father who dwells in me* does his works. Believe me that *I am in the Father and the Father*

is in me, or else believe on account of the works themselves (John 14:9-11).

In chapter 2, I wrote that the great horror of the cross was that Jesus would be separated from his Father. Now you can understand a little more just how painful this separation would be for Jesus. For all of eternity before the cross, the Father was in him and he was in the Father. As Jesus hanged from the cross, their separation meant severing this mutually indwelling relationship; it meant ripping apart a connection that went down to the very core of who Jesus was. This is a relationship so close, so intimate, so deep, that we cannot comprehend it, much less try to explain it.

And this is the kind of relationship that God pursues with us. Not content to adopt us, not content to betroth us, God chooses to indwell us.

This indwelling starts with the coming of the Holy Spirit, something Jesus told his disciples about in that upper room.

> If you love me, you will keep my commandments. And I will ask the Father, and he will give you another Helper, to be with you forever, even the Spirit of truth, whom the world cannot receive, because it neither sees him nor knows him. You know him, for he dwells with you *and will be in you*. (John 14:15-17).

Then, on the day of Pentecost that followed Jesus's ascension, Jesus's promise of the coming of the Holy Spirit was fulfilled:

The Relationship of Deep Prayer

When the day of Pentecost arrived, they were all together in one place. And suddenly there came from heaven a sound like a mighty rushing wind, and it filled the entire house where they were sitting. And divided tongues as of fire appeared to them and rested on each one of them. *And they were all filled with the Holy Spirit* and began to speak in other tongues as the Spirit gave them utterance (Acts 2:1-4).

The tongues of fire were the physical manifestation of the coming Spirit, but we're told that the Spirit didn't merely rest upon each of these disciples, but filled each one of them. The Holy Spirit, the other Helper, didn't come merely to be with them, but came to dwell inside them, just as Jesus had promised.

The rest of the New Testament shows us the blessing of having this indwelling relationship with the Spirit of God. It's the Spirit who gives us life (John 6:63); he teaches us (John 14:26); he guides us into truth (John 16:13); he love us (Romans 15:30); his dwelling inside us is how God's love is poured into our hearts (Romans 5:5); he intercedes for us (Romans 8:26); he fills us with hope (Romans 15:13); he bears witness to our adoption as sons (Romans 8:15; Galatians 4:6); and he is the seal and down payment of our eternal inheritance (Ephesians 1:13-14; 2 Corinthians 1:22, 5:5). Since he is the *Holy* Spirit, we are made holy through his work inside us (Romans 8:9-13; 2 Thessalonians 2:13; 1 Peter 1:1-2) and the fruits of this relationship give us a righteous character (Galatians 5:22-23). "In a word, all that believers have from grace to glory—all that they are from the first moment they believe to the day they depart to be with Christ—all, all, all may be traced to the work of the Holy Ghost."[25]

Back to the Garden

At the end of chapter 2, we asked whether Jesus's prayer in Gethsemane could be a model prayer for us since Jesus is God and we are just sinful creatures. Now we know that the Triune God pursues an intimacy with us which, although not the same as Jesus's relationship with his Father, is at least analogous with it. God pursues with us the same kind of relationship that Jesus has with his Father, so Jesus's deepest prayer, prayed in his most painful moment, should be the kind of prayer we pray to our Father in heaven. In fact, this kind of deep prayer will greatly help us deepen the intimacy of these relationships.

God's Definition vs. Personal Experience

God defines the relationship we can have with him, and we experience our own relationship with him as we live day by day. But, what if our experience doesn't match God's definition? What if the Christian life we're living doesn't look anything like the intimacy with God that he is pursuing?

---

[25] J. C. Ryle, "The Holy Ghost," in *Old Paths* (Edinburgh, Banner of Truth Trust, 1878, 1999), 269.

The Relationship of Deep Prayer

As it turns out, that's normal. When we get to heaven, we will have the exact kind of relationship—with all the parent-child closeness, all the husband-wife intimacy, and all the mutual indwelling transcendence—that God is pursuing with us right now. While we're on this earth, however, there will always be a gap between God's definition and our experience.

So, now what do we do? One approach would be to compare these biblical definitions to our own pitiful experience and feel convicted—or even condemned—for not measuring up. A biblical approach, however, would be to think deeply about how God has defined his relationship with us, compare it to our own reality, and then do what we can to grow our experience toward that definition.

During the Last Supper, Jesus told his disciples, "I am the vine; you are the branches" (John 15:5). This is a metaphor of our relationship with Jesus that matches the intimacy that we have already seen in this chapter: the Father adopts, the Son betroths, and the Spirit indwells. Branches are connected to their vines, they receive all their nutrition through this connection, and they bear fruit because of that nutrition. A branch that's not connected to the vine is just a dead piece of wood, destined to be "thrown into the fire, and burned" (John 15:6). The very thing that makes a branch a branch is its connection to the vine and yet, as Jesus talked to these branches, he commanded them and exhorted them and encouraged them to be a branch and abide in him. Like this: "Abide in me, and I in you. As the branch cannot bear fruit by itself, unless it abides in the vine, neither can you, unless you abide in me" (v. 4); "If you abide in me, and my words abide in you, ask whatever you wish, and it will be done for you" (v. 7); "As the Father has loved me, so have I loved you. Abide in my love" (v. 9). Jesus exhorted them to pursue in experience what God had given them by grace because he knows that this relationship grows over time, that there is always a gap between what God has for us and what we have received from him.

Paul understood this, too. When he prayed for the Christians in Ephesus, he told them he was asking God

> . . . that according to the riches of his glory he may grant you to be strengthened with power through his Spirit in your inner being, *so that Christ may dwell in your hearts through faith*—that you, being rooted and grounded in love, may have strength to comprehend with all the saints what is the breadth and length and height and depth, and to know the love of Christ that surpasses knowledge, that you may be filled with all the fullness of God (Ephesians 3:16-19).

Paul knew that Christ dwells in every heart that believes in him (2 Corinthians 13:5), and yet he prayed that the Ephesians would have the strength to have Christ dwell in their hearts. He understood the difference between what God has done and what Christians experience.

But our experience (or lack of experience) in this divine relationship cannot change God's definition of the

The Relationship of Deep Prayer

relationship he pursues with us. Since the Father adopts you, no one (including you) can emancipate you from his family. Since Jesus betroths you, no one (including you) can break you up. Since the Holy Spirit indwells you, no one (including you) can exercise him from your soul. These relationships of father to son and of husband to wife describe our permanent *status*, not our individual *experience*. Take, for example, two married couples. One couple has a rocky marriage marked by poor communication, lack of trust, and little affection. The other couple has a deep and intimate relationship with one another filled with mutual respect, true love, and real pleasure in each another. Both couples have a completely different experience of marriage, but both are married. The kind of marriage they have doesn't affect their status of being married.

If your relationship experience with God doesn't match the one described in the Bible, it doesn't mean you are not the Father's child, Jesus's bride, or the Spirit's temple. The answer isn't to dismiss the truth of the status because it doesn't match your experience; the answer is to bring your experience up to the status that's been revealed to you by God himself.

This is where deep prayer comes in.

We need to pray deep prayers to God regularly and intentionally so that we can experience the relationship God has for us. When we pray deep prayers, we're pursuing a relationship with God that reaches up to the status we were given on the day the righteous Judge exonerated us in Jesus. In the next chapter, I will teach you how the intimacy of this relationship God pursues with you should shape the way you talk to God—how deep prayer uses the language of intimacy: openness, honesty, sincerity, and even frankness, rashness, and intensity.

CHAPTER 4

THE LANGUAGE OF DEEP PRAYER

Language is amazingly flexible and versatile. We regularly change the way we talk based on the situation we're in: who we're talking to, the topic under discussion, and the goal we're pursuing in the conversation. I speak differently, using different words, a different tone, and different expressions, to my clients than I do to my colleagues; I talk differently to the guy who fixes my car than I do to my doctor; I talk differently to my neighbors than I do to the members of my church; I talk differently to my friends—even my closest friends—than I do to my wife and children. But we also talk differently to the same people when our situation or purpose changes. The conversation I have with my neighbor catching up on his work or his family is different from the one I have with him about a problem with the boundary line between our houses. I speak to my friends differently about Sunday's game than I do about a serious problem one of us is having. I spoke to my kids differently when I played with them than I did when I had to discipline them.

DEEP PRAYER

We all do this, automatically, instinctively, even unconsciously, as we go through our day. It's the kind of skill that keeps us from cracking jokes at a funeral or from spreading sadness at a wedding. But the key to using this skill is understanding the situation you're in and the relationship you have with the people you're talking to. If you misjudge this, you will end up using the wrong language. Admittedly, in most cases, this would be nothing more than a temporary embarrassment. But, if you have the wrong idea about your relationship with God, you could use the wrong language for years when talking to him, and that's a mistake that could seriously impact how you experience your relationship with him.

For most of my life, preachers and teachers have told me that, when I went to God in prayer, I was approaching the throne of a great king. They taught this because they were concerned that if I didn't understand the gravity of the situation I was in, I would use language that was common or frivolous, or even disrespectful. "You cannot talk to God like he's one of your friends," they would preach. Frequently that bit of instruction would be bolstered with a powerful illustration that sounded something like this:

Imagine you've been invited to meet the President of the United States in the Oval Office. Let's even assume that you didn't vote for him and that, when you talk politics with your friends, you criticize both the man and his policies in (to put it gently) unguarded language. Maybe, as the day

The Language of Deep Prayer

approaches, you have ideas about what you're going to say to him, how you're going to give him a piece of your mind, how you're going to make sure he knows what the little people are thinking.

But then, as you're being driven down Pennsylvania Avenue, you see the White House for the first time and you're moved by your love of the country this house represents. As you go through one security checkpoint after another, you're struck by the seriousness of the moment. When you're ushered into the Oval Office, you're overwhelmed by the privilege you've been given. When the President himself walks in, you're awestruck into silence, you know you cannot speak unless spoken to, that you do not set the agenda for this conversation, and that—even if you're asked for your honest opinion (and you have the courage to give it)—you wouldn't use the language and the tone you use back home with your friends, but would express your opinion in a ceremonious way, using formal words, a reverential tone, and maybe even a flattering manner.

Then, once the preacher had painted this picture, the application from the lesser to the greater would be made: if that's how you would act toward the human leader of one country, how much more honor and respect should you show to the divine sovereign over the whole universe? Then he might back this up with some really weighty examples from the Bible that show how critical it is that we approach God properly. He could bring up the time when the Israelites encountered God on Mt. Sinai and were told they had to be extremely careful when approaching him: "Take care not to go up into the mountain or touch the edge of it. Whoever *touches* the mountain *shall be put to death*" (Exodus 19:12); or the time when the sons of Aaron made offerings in the tabernacle for the first time and presented "unauthorized fire before the LORD, which he had not commanded them" and they were killed right on the spot (Leviticus 10:1-3); or the time King Saul made an offering to God that only priests were supposed to make, and God took the kingdom away from him (1 Samuel 13:5-15); or he might bring up what happened to another king, Uzziah, a faithful king who "did what was right in the eyes of the LORD," but who, toward the end of his reign, went into the temple to offer incense—something kings were forbidden to do—and God struck him with leprosy (2 Chronicles 26:16-21). After hearing all that, the warning would be clear: how dare you approach God lightly, flippantly, casually, commonly.

If you were taught to pray like I was, if you were taught that you were approaching a high and distant King from whom you seek help in trouble, then you have probably been using the language that fits this situation. When you ask a great king for help, you speak the formal language of the royal court, language designed to flatter the king as you to present your petitions before him, hoping to grab his interest so that he will act favorably on your request.

The Language of Deep Prayer

But what if, when you pray, you're *not* approaching a king in his throne room or the President in the Oval Office, but you're talking to your Father while sitting in the family room? What if the formal, careful, courtly language you have been using in your prayers is completely inappropriate to the situation you're in when you pray?

The Situation of Deep Prayer

The truth is, when those preachers told me to approach God carefully—even fearfully—like I would approach a great and powerful king, they were wrong. Not about God being a king or about God being great and powerful, but about the situation I as in when I prayed. The situation we're in whenever we pray is much more intimate and relational than that illustration implied. I have been describing that situation throughout the book: In chapter 1, I defined deep prayer as a conversation with a person inside a relationship. In chapter 2, we heard the language, tone, and expressions of the deepest prayer ever prayed. And in chapter 3, we discovered that God has defined his relationship with us in the most intimate terms we can understand—the Father adopts, the Son betroths, and the Spirit indwells. Bringing these lessons together, it turns out that the situation we're in when we pray is not a formal setting designed to intimidate, but a family setting of growing intimacy.

Once we understand that situation, then we need to start using the language appropriate to a family setting. That's why the question of how I would speak to the President of the United States if I was invited to the White House becomes irrelevant to how I should pray to God. The real question is, how do the President's *children* talk to him while sitting in the family room of their private home? In the family room, his children do not use the formal, stilted, polite language and careful protocol of the Oval Office; they speak to their own father honestly,[26] with openness, vulnerability, sincerity, and frankness suited to the relationship they have. This language of growing intimacy is the language of deep prayer. Therefore, deep payer is any prayer—from a poetic song of high praise to a wordless groan in terrible grief—that pursues a growing intimacy with God.

This is a long chapter, but it's also the most important. In this chapter, you will learn how to pray deep prayers to God regularly and intentionally by always using this language of growing intimacy. The language of deep prayer is whatever words you have inside you when you talk to God about what's on your mind and soul. The language of deep

---

[26] In the context of relationships, the opposite of honesty isn't lying, it's hiding. Jesus's prayer is honest because he told his Father about his pain instead of hiding it from him; because he told his Father he was overwhelmed instead of pretending he was fine with it; because he cried out for help in his pain instead of praising his Father for sending him on his mission.

The Language of Deep Prayer

prayer might include the most impressive words you know in an attempt to express your awe at God's greatness or your gratitude for his blessings; or it might be the groans you spit out in pain because you cannot find any words at all. It might be a carefully crafted argument rooted in thoughtful reflection or it could be rough words strung together to make incoherent sentences in the spur of the moment.

Most Christians I have talked to about this have no problem using their biggest, most impressive vocabulary or crafting careful arguments when they pray, but they have a hard time with the groans and the incoherence. So, as I teach you the language of deep prayer in this chapter, I'm not going to focus on the many prayers in the Bible that praise God in majestic poetry, I'm going to focus on the prayers recorded in the Bible that cry out to God in real pain. I'm doing this because the prayers of deep pain tend to be emotional, harsh, blunt, and even insolent—the kind of language that might make you squirm. But God put these prayers in his Word to reveal to us just how much he values our honesty and openness and sincerity and to let us know that the kind of language a king might punish is the very language a father welcomes. By the time you finish this chapter, you should be much more free to talk to God just the way you are, using your own words that flow out of whatever you're going through at the time. The language of deep prayer is *your* words spoken to *your* Father in *your* situation. Choosing this language every time you talk to God is how you pray deep prayers to God regularly and intentionally.

The Model Prayer: Jesus in the Garden

When Jesus was in the garden that night, facing the horrors of his upcoming crucifixion, he was a Son in pain talking to his Father. Since he understood the situation he was in, he didn't have to calm himself down, or dress up his request, or even make a reasoned argument for his position; he simply cried out to his Father with the words that expressed the anguish he was feeling in that moment, just before he was separated from his Father for the first time. He told his Father how he felt and what he wanted because he felt that way. Since this is our model for deep prayer, we can do the same thing. We can talk to God using whatever words we need to express our thoughts and emotions—whether joy, grief, pain, gratitude, confusion, frustration, pleasure, or sorrow. Praying deep prayers regularly and intentionally means talking to God without restrictive filters, without stilted formality, without empty flattery. You can simply talk to God as yourself, as you really are and you really feel, not like how you think you're supposed to be and supposed to feel.

The Example of Job

The story of Job is one of the more fascinating stories in the Bible. The outline of that story is well known: Job was the richest and most respected man in his day; on a single, horrible day, he lost all his wealth and had to bury all ten of his children; then, on a different day of increased suffering, he contracted a disease that produced painful, oozing sores all over his body; and yet, in the immediate aftermath of these losses, Job remained faithful to God (that is, he never cursed God for taking everything away from him). All of that happens in the first two chapters and can lead us to assume that Job's great trial was the loss of his money, family, and health and that the great lesson we learn from Job's life is that it's possible to respond to such a trial with faith and trust.

There is a lot of truth in that. After all, for Job to have responded with faith in the very moment of his sweeping losses meant that he had thought deeply about the ultimate source of his prosperity, about "the uncertainty of riches" (1 Timothy 6:17), and even about how he would react if God took it all away. However, as you dig deeper into the story, you will find that all these crushing losses were the introduction to a deeper crisis in Job's faith that shook his relationship with God down to its foundation. While he was living every day with the pain and grief, his losses also forced him to face an impossible conclusion: the God he had loved and trusted had turned away from him, and his faithful friend had become a powerful enemy.

Job was forced to face that conclusion because, in his day, the commonly held belief about God was that he rewards faithfulness and punishes wickedness. This, of course, is a biblical idea (see 2 Corinthians 9:6; Galatians 6:7), but the theologians of Job's day had twisted this in two ways. First, they believed that these rewards and punishments were meted out by God in this life, almost in real time. Second, they believed that you could tell who was righteous and who was sinning by measuring their level of prosperity. So, while Job and his family were wealthy and healthy, the consensus was that he was faithful to God but, as soon as Job lost everything, the consensus immediately shifted, and people then knew that Job was a great sinner.

Job believed this, too. If what had happened to him had happened to someone else, he would have agreed with the consensus opinion that this man must have been a great sinner. But, at the beginning of the book, we're given God's own testimony about Job, that he was "a blameless and upright man, who fears God and turns away from evil" and that "there is none like him on the earth" (Job 1:8). This was just as true of Job after he lost everything as it was before. Actually, it was *because* this was true of Job that he lost everything (Job 1:8-12). Since Job knew he had not sinned against God, and since Job thought God prospered the faithful and punished sinners, Job concluded that God was treating him like a sinner—like a great sinner, in fact—making God unrighteous and unjust in his treatment of Job. Job thought that God had not only turned against him, but that God had also turned against his own righteous character. The story the book of Job tells is about Job's reaction to this

The Language of Deep Prayer

deeper struggle, to this crisis of faith in Job's life.

We know that Job had an intimate relationship with God before he lost everything because of God's own testimony and commendation of Job. To have such an intimate relationship with God indicates that Job had a long practice of deep prayer, something that didn't change after his trial started. All of Job's prayers recorded throughout the book are deep prayers, they are prayers seeking God, trying to understand God, and expressing his anguish at losing his connection to God. Take a look at the first prayer Job prayed after all this suffering came out of nowhere and tore him away from the God he loved:

> After this Job opened his mouth and cursed the day of his birth. And Job said:
> "Let the day perish on which I was born,
>   and the night that said,
>   'A man is conceived.'
> Let that day be darkness!
>   May God above not seek it,
>   nor light shine upon it.
> Let gloom and deep darkness claim it.
>   Let clouds dwell upon it;
>   let the blackness of the day terrify it.
> That night—let thick darkness seize it!
>   Let it not rejoice among the days of the year;
>   let it not come into the number of the months.
> Behold, let that night be barren;
>   let no joyful cry enter it" (Job 3:1-7).

Have you ever known someone who was so sorrowful,

so grief-stricken, that he wished he had never been born? We understand what he means, too. He means that his trauma is so horrible that, even if you added up all the good he has ever experienced in his life—all his comforts, his closest relationships, his greatest successes, and all his joys—his life would still not have been worth living. Later in this prayer, Job expressed that kind of grief when he cried out, "Why did I not die at birth, come out from the womb and expire?" (verse 11). Since Job had experienced more blessings than most of us could ever imagine, this tells us just how terrible this trial was to him.

But wishing he hadn't been born still wasn't enough to express the depth of grief, pain, and trauma Job was going through, so in these first words of prayer, he cursed not just his birth, but the day he was born. His pain was so great, that it wasn't enough that he never existed, he wanted his birthday to cease existing, too. Job is thinking like an ancient marauder who went around conquering one city after another—until he came to a city that he really hated, a city that had betrayed or abused him. It wouldn't be enough to merely to conquer this place and carry away their wealth; he also had to kill all the people, burn all the buildings, and scrape the ashes into the ocean—to make it so that the city no longer existed. In the same way, Job wanted his birthday to perish, to be covered in darkness, gloom, and a terrifying blackness. He wanted to deny it a place on the calendar so that no joyful cry could ever be uttered on that day.

The Language of Deep Prayer

This is strong, hard, tormented language that Job was free to use as he cried out in his grief. Job was so close to God that he could talk to him with this kind of openness and honesty. That's the language of deep prayer.

Later in Job's ordeal, he prayed again. Although he is still suffering and still confused and frustrated, in this later prayer, he is trying to be more reasonable. However, he still asks God for an outrageous concession:

> Only grant me two things,
> > then I will not hide myself from your face:
> withdraw your hand far from me,
> > and let not dread of you terrify me.
> Then call, and I will answer;
> > or let me speak, and you reply to me.
> How many are my iniquities and my sins?
> > Make me know my transgression and my sin.
> Why do you hide your face
> > and count me as your enemy?
> Will you frighten a driven leaf
> > and pursue dry chaff? (Job 13:20-25).

Job asks God to come to him so that Job can question him! Job wants God to list out his iniquities and sins, presumably so he can defend himself against these charges. He also accuses God of hiding from Job and counting him as God's enemy. This is just as deep a prayer as the first one quoted above, but Job held his emotions in check while he searched for a solution to his trial. But this prayer also shows just how free Job was to speak his mind to God. The irony is that Job's trial will end when God does just as Job asked, and presents himself to Job. However, Job will not be the one asking the questions. Instead, God will examine Job—specifically his knowledge and wisdom of things in the world—as a way of revealing the full depth of God's wisdom and knowledge to Job. It was in that revelation that Job finally learned that God never treated him like a sinner, that Job's ideas about God, sin, and suffering were wrong, and that God's ways in the world are far more complex than Job's simple theology allowed.

By using the open and honest language of deep prayer, then, Job was moving closer to God through his trial and (without knowing it) was preparing his soul for when God would speak to him and teach him greater things about himself.

Examples in Psalms

The book of Psalms is the prayer book of the Bible, a collection of all kinds of prayers to God that can show us how to pray in any situation we find ourselves. About one-third of those prayers are classified as lament psalms: prayers that are prayed in some kind of pain or grief or sorrow. God graciously preserved these prayers in his Word to teach us the language of deep prayer and to show that he listens to open and honest prayers, even when they express pain, confusion, frustration, and anger in harsh and bitter words. I have chosen the three prayers below because they

The Language of Deep Prayer

all, at their core, express distress over the psalmist's relationship with God. In all three prayers, something bad had happened that the psalmist expected God to prevent or correct but, instead of intervening, God let it happen. The pain they express is partly over the circumstances they are in but mostly over the grief that God didn't show up to help as they expected.

1. Psalm 74. In my first example, the psalmist's pain is caused by outward circumstances—in this case the destruction of Solomon's temple by the Babylonians. In his pain, the psalmist doesn't blame Israelite unfaithfulness, or even Babylonian ruthlessness, for this horrible act, he blames God:

> O God, why do you cast us off forever?
>> Why does your anger smoke against the sheep of your pasture?
> Remember your congregation,
>> which you have purchased of old,
>> which you have redeemed to be the tribe of your heritage!
> Remember Mount Zion, where you have dwelt.
> Direct your steps to the perpetual ruins;
>> the enemy has destroyed everything in the sanctuary!
>> (Psalm 74:1-3)

The temple built by the great King Solomon was an architectural wonder and the pride of Israel, but it was also the spiritual center of the people of God because the temple was where God dwelt among his people. Seeing an enemy army tear it down was the equivalent of seeing God defeated and evicted. Since nothing can defeat God, the psalmist's mind was flooded with the worst possible thought: God let this happen to us! God abandoned us! God has rejected us! The circumstances may have been bitter, but the idea that God had forgotten them was crushing. The first words that spill out in his grief do not focus on the circumstances, but on God's absence.

As he throws himself down to his knees, he asks God how he can be so angry that he cast his own people away from him. Then, looking at the smoldering ruins of God's great temple, he begs God to remember Mount Zion, where the temple was located. God knows everything and forgets nothing, so asking him to remember isn't a request that he recall to his mind some lost fact; rather it's a plea that God would get up off his throne and actively engage in the world by doing what he promised.

Don't smooth off the rough edges of this brutally direct and honest prayer; don't sanitize the pain and grief expressed here. The psalmist was looking out at death and destruction and couldn't understand why God wasn't there when his chosen people needed him, why God didn't defend them against their enemies, why God had abandoned his covenant promises, why God had stayed away from Jerusalem and refused to look at the results of his unconscionable neglect.

The Language of Deep Prayer

This prayer isn't completely dark. At some point[27] in his great grief, the psalmist remembered who God is and this memory formed the basis of the prayer that comes at the end of the psalm.

> Yet God my King is from old,
> > working salvation in the midst of the earth.
> You divided the sea by your might;
> > you broke the heads of the sea monsters on the waters.
> You crushed the heads of Leviathan;
> > you gave him as food for the creatures of the wilderness.
> You split open springs and brooks;
> > you dried up ever-flowing streams.
> Yours is the day; yours also the night;
> > you have established the heavenly lights and the sun.
> You have fixed all the boundaries of the earth;
> > you have made summer and winter (vv. 12-17).

The psalmist recognized God as the King who had done

---

[27]"The psalms are poetic compositions; some were no doubt composed orally and spontaneously, whereas others were literary compositions in a more formal sense." Peter C. Craigie and Marvin E. Tate, *Psalms 1-50, Word Biblical Commentary*, v. 19 (NP, Thomas Nelson, Inc., 2004), 35. The psalms that are literary compositions were written over time and reflected back, not on a single moment of prayer, but on a journey of prayer that started with pain and moved into renewed faith. That's an important point because it means we don't have to imagine that the psalmist's grief over the loss of both the temple and the nation wrung itself out in the few minutes it takes us to read 11 verses.

these mighty acts of creation and salvation and, because he remembered all that, he knew could make his requests to God while standing in the middle of a ruined city. However, his requests still mirror the complaints he made at the beginning of the psalm. So, while his requests were now more focused, he was still praying honestly through his pain:

> Have regard for the covenant,
> > for the dark places of the land are full of the habitations of violence.
> Let not the downtrodden turn back in shame;
> > let the poor and needy praise your name.
>
> Arise, O God, defend your cause;
> > remember how the foolish scoff at you all the day!
> Do not forget the clamor of your foes,
> > the uproar of those who rise against you, which goes up continually! (vv. 18-23).

2. Psalm 44. The prayers of Jesus in the garden, Job's first prayer in his trial, and Psalm 74 were all prayed in the throes of churning emotions over catastrophic circumstances. But what happens after the wave of emotion has swept by? Can you still pray deep prayers? Of course! Deep prayers are relational prayers that can take on whatever emotion or style or words that you need to express yourself in your changing situation—prayers that seek God and pursue a deeper relationship with him in every and any circumstance.

Psalm 44 is prayed after the emotional wave has passed

and the psalmist has had a chance to reflect on the disaster he has seen. He also prayed about Israel's defeat in battle (we don't know which battle) and prayed through what happened and why. Unlike our previous examples of deep prayer, this psalm doesn't record the first words the psalmist blurted out in his grief; instead, it records the words the psalmist prayed after he had thought through his grief. This prayer is even more brutal because he expressed it as a reasoned argument against God and an indictment of God's failure to act for the nation and the people. As he brought his case against God, the psalmist started out by recounting what God had done for Israel in the past:

> O God, we have heard with our ears,
>   our fathers have told us,
>   what deeds you performed in their days,
>   in the days of old:
>   you with your own hand drove out the nations,
>   but them you planted;
>   you afflicted the peoples,
>   but them you set free;
>   for not by their own sword did they win the land,
>   nor did their own arm save them,
>   but your right hand and your arm,
>   and the light of your face,
>   for you delighted in them (Psalm 44:1-3).

The psalmist told God that his people had heard the stories of how God acted for the people of Israel in the past, here recounting specifically the days of Moses, when God afflicted the Egyptians with plagues to set Israel free, and the days of Joshua, when God drove out powerful nations and planted Israel in the land. He acknowledged that this small nation didn't have the military might to do this, but that it was done by God's right hand and arm. But not just by his hand and arm. God did this for them by "the light of your face, for you delighted in them" (v. 3). God's power could save anyone; they were saved by that power because God loved them.

The second step in his argument was that these past actions had instilled confidence and faith in God within the current generation of his people:

> You are my King, O God;
>   ordain salvation for Jacob!
> Through you we push down our foes;
>   through your name we tread down those who rise up
>   against us.
> For not in my bow do I trust,
>   nor can my sword save me.
> But you have saved us from our foes
>   and have put to shame those who hate us.
> In God we have boasted continually,
>   and we will give thanks to your name forever
>   (vv. 4-8).

Isn't this exactly how it's supposed to work? God loves the people, the people trust in God, God acts to save the people from their foes, the people then give thanks to God forever. According to this psalmist, God had held up his end in the past, the people were holding up their end in the

The Language of Deep Prayer

present, but then God failed them:

> But you have rejected us and disgraced us
>   and have not gone out with our armies.
> You have made us turn back from the foe,
>   and those who hate us have gotten spoil.
> You have made us like sheep for slaughter
>   and have scattered us among the nations.
> You have sold your people for a trifle,
>   demanding no high price for them
> (vv. 9-12).

This is the climax of the argument. After laying out his case, the psalmist's pain comes bursting out. He cried out, Oh God, you could have defeated them! You *should have* defeated them! You could have shown the world your power and strength by using our powerless nation to defeat a powerful enemy! We needed you and you abandoned us! You slaughtered your own people! The pain in this prayer is that the God they knew, the God they had heard so much about, the God they trusted, wasn't there when they needed him. The pain in this prayer is that it looked like God abandoned his promises. The pain in this prayer is that it felt like God had sold them out at a bargain price.

But that only expresses part of the pain. The psalmist's pain runs even deeper as he recalls the faithfulness of the nation:

> All this has come upon us,
>   though we have not forgotten you,
>   and we have not been false to your covenant.

> Our heart has not turned back,
> > nor have our steps departed from your way;
> yet you have broken us in the place of jackals
> > and covered us with the shadow of death.
> If we had forgotten the name of our God
> > or spread out our hands to a foreign god,
> would not God discover this?
> > For he knows the secrets of the heart.
> Yet for your sake we are killed all the day long;
> > we are regarded as sheep to be slaughtered (vv. 17-22).

The accusations here are subtle, but they are powerful: "we have not forgotten you" implies God is the one who has forgotten; "we have not been false to your covenant" implies that God is the one who has been false. This prayer may have been sparked by Israel's defeat in battle, but the pain in the prayer is what the psalmist saw as a break in their relationship with God. It's this pain-filled perspective that leads to the blunt, coarse, and honest demands made at the end of the prayer:

> Awake! Why are you sleeping, O Lord?
> > Rouse yourself! Do not reject us forever!
> Why do you hide your face?
> > Why do you forget our affliction and oppression?
> For our soul is bowed down to the dust;
> > our belly clings to the ground.
> Rise up; come to our help!
> > Redeem us for the sake of your steadfast love! (vv. 23-26).

The Language of Deep Prayer

This is the kind of prayer God welcomes from his children. I included this psalm because I don't want to give the impression that God tolerates rough language from his people because he knows their pain has clouded their thinking. In this psalm, the emotional signature is completely different, so the rough language and blunt requests come after careful thought and theological reflection, and yet God still encourages his children to speak the language of honest, open, and authentic prayers—prayers that seek him even when the one praying cannot see him or find him and wonders where he is.

3. Psalm 88. My third example comes from the darkest and most hopeless prayer in the entire Bible. The prayer is complaint, pain, and grief from beginning to end. This prayer has the same blunt, raw, direct language used in the previous examples, but I'm using this not just as an example of the honest and open language of deep prayer but also to show you how the language of deep prayer flows out of a deep relationship with God.

> Here is how the prayer starts:
> O LORD, God of my salvation,
>   I cry out day and night before you.
> Let my prayer come before you;
>   incline your ear to my cry!
>
> For my soul is full of troubles,
>   and my life draws near to Sheol.
> I am counted among those who go down to the pit;
>   I am a man who has no strength,

> like one set loose among the dead, like the slain
> that lie in the grave,
> like those whom you remember no more,
> > for they are cut off from your hand
> > (Psalm 88:3-5).

As dark as this opening is, this prayer only gets darker when the psalmist blames God for his suffering:

> You have put me in the depths of the pit,
> > in the regions dark and deep.
> Your wrath lies heavy upon me,
> > and you overwhelm me with all your waves.
>
> You have caused my companions to shun me;
> > you have made me a horror to them.
> I am shut in so that I cannot escape;
> > my eye grows dim through sorrow.
> > (vv. 6-9a).

These accusations don't let up, either. After a series of questions about death, he again accuses God of putting him in this painful state:

> O Lord, why do you cast my soul away?
> > Why do you hide your face from me?
> Afflicted and close to death from my youth up,
> > I suffer your terrors; I am helpless.
> Your wrath has swept over me,
> > your dreadful assaults destroy me.
> They surround me like a flood all day long;
> > they close in on me together.
> You have caused my beloved and my friend to shun me;

The Language of Deep Prayer

> my companions have become darkness
> (vv. 14-18).

This is a dark prayer, but the darkness in this prayer actually shows us just how deep this man's relationship with God was. Since the language of deep prayer is openness, authenticity, honesty, and sincerity, I think the level of the psalmist's openness and honesty reveals a very deep relationship with God. Consider, first, what the psalmist is praying for. Throughout the psalm, we can see there is a lot of bad stuff going on in this man's life. He feels like God has abandoned him—is even punishing him—as he suffers great distress from his circumstances. I'm sure there must have been dozens and dozens of things he could have asked God to do for him, but in this psalm of complaint and lament, he only asks God for one thing: "Let my prayer come before you; incline your ear to my cry!" (v. 2). He didn't ask God to change his circumstances; he didn't ask that his friends come back to him and support him; he didn't even ask God to take away his pain and anguish. Instead, he asked God to connect with his soul once again. In Psalm 23, David wrote, "Even though I walk through the valley of the shadow of death, I will fear no evil, for you are with me; your rod and your staff, they comfort me" (v. 4). The man who prayed Psalm 88 was going through the valley of the shadow of death without God being with him, without any comfort from God. He didn't ask God to take him out of the valley, he asked God to start walking with him again. This man understood that his greatest need was God himself, and that shows he had a deep relationship with God.

The second way I know this man had a deep relationship with God is the depth of his grief over the depth of his loss. As we read through this psalm, we can feel this man's grief, and deep grief means the loss of a deep relationship. For example, if a distant acquaintance dropped out of your life, how much different would your life be from day to day? Sure, you may miss her but, because you weren't that close, you just move on with your life. If God had been a distant acquaintance of this psalmist, he could never have prayed a prayer like Psalm 88. He simply wouldn't have missed God enough to grieve over his absence like that.

But what if your spouse dies? This relationship is much more intimate, so it disrupts everything in your life, not just the day-to-day but the minute-to-minute. Missing your spouse is painful and you grieve over the loss for years. That's the kind of intimate relationship the psalmist had to have with God to lament with such intense grief and sorrow over what he perceived as God's distance from him.

Finally, the psalmist shows the depth of his relationship with God by the accusations he makes throughout his prayer. Read though the psalm again and underline how many times he uses the words "you" or "your." Like in verse 6 when he says, "*You* have put me in the depths of the pit" or in verse 16: "*your* dreadful assaults destroy me." At first glance, this sounds like the psalmist is accusing God of being an evil enemy, like he is screaming at the sky while shaking his fist at God, charging him with fault and wrongdoing. A second look, however, reveals the depth of the relationship this man had with God. Instead of blaming God, he acknowledged that God stood behind everything that happened to him. While praying this prayer, the psalmist swept from his mind a score of secondary causes that had attacked him and locked onto the primary cause, the ultimate mover of all events in the universe, standing behind it all. Instead of seeing his troubles as a series of random events, instead of focusing on the malice or stupidity of others, instead of thinking his pain had no meaning, he saw his best friend standing there. Only someone with a deep and intimate relationship with God can see him standing there in the darkest moments; only someone with a deep and intimate relationship with God could feel both the pain of the circumstances and the love of the Father at the same time.

The language of deep prayer is openness, honesty, and authenticity. Using this language will help you deepen your relationship with God (more on that in the next chapter). But deepening the relationship will also make this kind of language easier to use.

Encouragements to Deep Prayers

The prayers of Jesus, Job, and these psalms teach us, by example, the language of deep prayer. These examples are valuable, even essential, because we get to hear real prayers from real people in real relationships with God. But God doesn't just teach us by example; he also tells us straight out to use the language of deep prayer that we have just heard. He does that by exhorting—even commanding—us to bring all our requests, all our anxieties, all our concerns straight to him in the open and honest language of deep prayer.

1. Philippians 4:6: When Paul wrote to the church at Philippi, he told them that the antidote to anxiety is deep prayer: "do not be anxious about anything, but in everything by prayer and supplication with thanksgiving let your requests be made known to God" (Philippians 4:6). The word "everything" in this verse means "everything": our pain, our burdens, our anxieties, our suffering, our frustration, our anger. God wants to hear it all—our grumbling and our gratitude, our general prayers and specific requests. He isn't concerned about the formalities of our prayers; he just wants us to pray about everything in our lives, and that requires us to use the language of honesty and openness.

2. The Book of Hebrews: The book of Hebrews was written to Jewish Christians living in the first century (probably before 70 A.D.) who were being pulled back into Judaism: back to their families, back to their communities, back to the synagogue, back to the temple, back to the old rituals, back to the old sacrifices, back to the old covenant. To encourage them to hold fast, the writer of Hebrews

The Language of Deep Prayer

pointed them to Jesus: Jesus is superior to angels (chapters 1-2), Jesus is greater than Moses (chapter 3), Jesus is the great high priest (chapters 5-7), of a better covenant (chapter 8), with a better sacrifice (chapter 9).

At the end of chapter 4, as the writer is about to teach about Jesus as the great high priest, he writes about each Christian's access to God through this high priest:

> Since then we have a great high priest who has passed through the heavens, Jesus, the Son of God, let us hold fast our confession. For we do not have a high priest who is unable to sympathize with our weaknesses, but one who in every respect has been tempted as we are, yet without sin. Let us then with confidence draw near to the throne of grace, that we may receive mercy and find grace to help in time of need (Hebrews 4:14-16).

In Judaism, only the currently serving high priest had access to God's "throne of grace," and only on one day each year. But through Jesus, every Christian has continual access through prayer to the grace and mercy that flows from God to his people.[28] Because Jesus opened up for us this

---

[28]"The force of the present tense . . . is 'let us again and again draw near to the throne of grace.' . . . In a bold extension of the language of worship the writer calls the community to recognize that through his high priestly ministry Christ has achieved for them what Israel never enjoyed, namely immediate access to God and the freedom to draw near to him continually. They may draw near to God through prayer with the confidence that they will be graciously received" (citations omitted). William L. Lane, *Hebrews 1-8, Word Biblical Commentary*, vol. 47A (Dallas, Word Books, 1991), 115.

unprecedented access to God, we are encouraged to draw near to God "with confidence." This word carries with it the idea of freedom—freedom to speak our mind boldly, frankly, and openly.[29] Because Jesus is our great high priest, we are encouraged to talk to the Father at any time using whatever words we need to express ourselves.

Then, in chapter 10, after the writer has described the high priesthood of Jesus, along with the better covenant Jesus mediates and the better sacrifice Jesus made for us, he again describes our full and free access to God:

> Therefore, brothers, since we have confidence to enter the holy places by the blood of Jesus, by the new and living way that he opened for us through the curtain, that is, through his flesh, and since we have a great priest over the house of God, let us draw near with a true heart in full assurance of faith, with our hearts sprinkled clean from an evil conscience and our bodies washed with pure water (Hebrews 10:19-22).

The freedom to approach the Father frequently and frankly is ours not only because Jesus is the great high priest, but also because, through his sacrificial death, he tore open the curtain to the holy places. In this passage, however, the freedom to approach God is assumed ("Therefore, *since we have confidence* to enter . . .") and the exhortation is to draw

---

[29]*The New International Dictionary of New Testament Theology*, vol. 2 (Grand Rapids, Zondervan Publishing House, 1981, 1976), 734-37.

The Language of Deep Prayer

near to God. Drawing near to God, deepening our relationship with God, is the goal of praying openly, honestly, and frankly every time we talk to God.

3. Psalm 55: In Psalm 55, David wrote, "But I call to God, and the LORD will save me. Evening and morning and at noon I utter my complaint and moan, and he hears my voice" (vv. 16-17). David had confidence that God heard his prayers, not only the many beautiful, poetic, carefully worded prayers of David recorded throughout the book of Psalms, but also his complaint, his moaning, and his anguish. Then, a few verses later, this confidence encouraged David to pray a certain kind of prayer: "Cast your burden on the LORD, and he will sustain you; he will never permit the righteous to be moved" (v. 22). The word "cast" means to throw something at God,[30] and the burden we're commanded to cast on the Lord is the circumstances of our life, the lot we have been given in life by God himself.[31] So, the Bible commands us to take whatever God has given us to endure in this life and throw it back up at him in prayer. David's deep relationship with God meant that he could pray whatever kind of prayer he needed to, using the words that

---

[30] Alec Motyer, *Psalms by the Day: A Working Translation with Analysis and Explanatory Notes, and a 'Pause for Thought' Based on the Passage Read* (Ross-shire, Scotland, Christian Focus Publications, Ltd, 2016), 146.

[31] Marvin E. Tate, *Psalms 51-100, Word Biblical Commentary*, vol. 20 (Nashville, Thomas Nelson, 1990), 58.

were appropriate in his situation—whether praise or moaning, whether the song of worship or the casting of burdens.

Objection: Fathers Deserve Respect, Too!

Maybe you agree with me that, although God is a great King, he is also your loving Father and that the Father-child relationship should define how you talk to him. But, you may also be thinking, your Father is still someone to be respected and you need to be careful how you talk to him. And I agree with you. Deep prayer is relational prayer, and the language of deep prayer will always be shaped by the relationship we have with God. So, while I have been showing you prayers that use blunt words to express powerful emotions, I do not want to give the impression that we can be insolent, rude, and obnoxious when we pray to God. We should have the deepest respect and honor for God whenever we pray, no matter what we're feeling. But if you have been trained to pray like a subject talking to a king, then you need to understand that the way we show respect to a father is different from the way we show respect for a king.

You respect a king by following protocol when speaking to him, by not wasting his time on trivial matters, by listening to him and not speaking unless spoken to, by using polite speech and proper words. But you respect a father by having a relationship with him, by telling him everything that's on your mind, by sharing yourself with him, by seeking his help when you need him, and by talking to him openly and sincerely.

When my youngest son came back from war, I was happy that he was alive and healthy, but I was concerned about the state of his soul. When we talked, he told me all was well, that he was seeking God, that he was doing just fine. Then one day, over a year after he was discharged from the Marines, he came and told me what was really going on, about all the ways his experience in war was wreaking havoc in his soul. He spoke bluntly about what he had seen, about the sin in his life, about how he was reacting to things around him. Now, let me ask you, which one of those behaviors, the hiding or the openness, do you think deepened our relationship as father and son?

That is the important question. Too often, when people warn against talking to God bluntly and emotionally—whether in pain or in joy—they focus on the words being used and how the requests are presented. Instead, the focus should be on what deepens our relationship with God. Since the Father adopted us, Jesus betrothed us, and the Spirit indwells us, the most honoring way we can pray is by pursuing a deeper relationship with our God. So, while the language of deep prayer isn't flippancy, arrogance, or insolence; and while there may be a fine line between being bluntly honest and rudely impertinent; and while we may cross that line from time to time in our prayers, that's not our greatest danger when we pray. God can handle, and he will lovingly correct, any disrespect we may inadvertently show him. That's what happened to Job. After God revealed himself to Job, Job realized that he had said a lot of stupid things during his trial, so he repented "in dust and ashes" (Job 42:6). But when God turned and spoke to one of Job's three friends, he rebuked him: "My anger burns against you and your two friends, for you have not spoken of me what is right, *as my servant Job has*" (v. 7). The very thing for which Job repented, God commended him for. That's because the greater danger in prayer is withholding your soul from God; it's not speaking rashly as you sincerely seek him in your deepest need and pain.

Learning to Speak the Language of Deep Prayer

Remember, I wrote this book to help you pray deep prayers to God regularly and intentionally. While I'm happy you decided to read this book, if all you do is read, then my mission will have failed. Therefore, as I end this most important chapter, I want to help you speak the language of deep prayer by addressing some of the hurdles you may be facing as you get started.

1. The Novelty Hurdle. You might be reading this chapter, after praying for many years, and may be happy that someone has put into words the things you've been thinking and feeling—maybe on the edges of your mind—for a while. If that's you, then I hope you will use this chapter to pray like this, to pray as God has been leading you to pray, regularly and intentionally.

For other readers, however, all of this may be brand new and you may be struggling with the novelty of it all. If that's you, I have one request: Please don't dismiss what I have written simply because it's new to you. Instead, I ask you to go through this chapter again, read carefully the Scriptures I have cited, study those verses in their contexts, and meditate on their meaning and application. While you're doing this, also talk to God about what you're thinking. Ask him whether he wants you to talk to him openly, honestly, authentically, and emotionally.

2. The Shock Hurdle. If you have been trained to use courtly language to talk to the King of kings, and you have always prayed careful and proper-sounding prayers to God, the language I have shown you in this chapter may not sound merely novel, but outright shocking to you. Maybe you're even thinking you could never talk to God like that.

It's true that the goal of deep prayer is to have such a deep relationship with God that you can tell him anything—everything!—that's on your mind at any time. But deep relationships grow over time. On your first day, you may not be able to cry out, like Job did, "I loathe my life; I would not live forever. Leave me alone, for my days are a breath" (Job 7:16). So, don't try! Simply talk to God as openly and honestly as you can. The difference may be subtle, and the language may be nearly indistinguishable from your prior prayers, but God, who sees your heart, will know the difference. In the next chapter, I will show you what God does with your deep prayers, even your first, halting attempts at it. This should encourage you that, as God works in your soul, you will become more and more comfortable speaking the language of deep prayer.

3. The Emotional Hurdle. As we went through the biblical examples of deep prayer, we heard a lot of different emotions expressed. We heard some raw anger, some calculated expressions of disappointment, some real frustration, and some strong defiance. Maybe, as you listened, your first thought was, "I could never talk to God with that kind of emotion"—whatever that emotion was. But remember, relationships are personal, so the goal is to be honest, open, and authentic, not to express a specific kind of emotion. Every person's emotional make-up is different, so the emotions expressed in each person's prayers will also be different. A person who tends to react to things with anger will show honest anger when he prays. Someone else, whose emotions turn toward the melancholy, will express distress or discouragement when praying a deep prayer. Others, who get easily frustrated by circumstances, will probably express confusion and exasperation in their deepest prayers. The point isn't to express every possible emotion when you pray, it's to be yourself, to be honest about the emotions you actually have. The prayers recorded in the Bible express a range of emotions, not because God expects you to express emotions you don't have, but to encourage you to talk to God no matter what emotions you actually have.

4. The Variety Hurdle. All the examples of deep prayer I used in this chapter have been laments, prayers prayed in pain or trial. Maybe you've been thinking about your own prayers and wondered about all the other kinds of prayers you pray: intercession, adoration, repentance, thanksgiving, praise, confession. Can all these kinds of prayers also be deep? Yes, they can and they should.

The language of deep prayer should be used no matter what kind of prayer you're praying. When you're happy, you should express your joy with true, raw emotion, allowing your expressions of praise to flow straight from your heart. When you're grateful for God's blessings, whether the great blessing of saving your soul or a smaller blessing of providing your daily bread, you should pray deep prayers of thanksgiving that express your true feelings of gratitude. When you're overwhelmed by the greatness, the majesty, the infinity of God, a deep prayer would be aflame with worship for who God is and how in awe of him you really are in that moment.

We can also pray deep prayers of repentance and confession. These can be hard because deep prayers of confession force us to look honestly at our sins before we confess them to God, and we often have a hard time doing that. But just start with where you are. Even if the most honest confession you can muster is, "It's not my fault!" then pray that. Like all things in the Christian life, honesty will grow over time. At some point, you will be able to admit you sinned and then, eventually, you will pray more deeply, confessing not just sinful behaviors but the sinfulness in your heart that fed that behavior. Jesus told us that "out of the heart come evil thoughts, murder, adultery, sexual immorality, theft, false witness, slander" (Matthew 15:19). As your relationship with God gets deeper, and your repentance bores deeper into your soul, these prayers will become, in the vivid words of one Puritan, "the vomit of the soul,"[32] the time when all the vile stuff that's down deep inside you comes up and is eliminated.

Your prayers for others can also be deep, not only because you can be authentic when sharing the burden you feel over the needs of others, but also because your primary request for everyone you pray for should be that they know God more deeply as they go through the trials and difficulties they need prayer about. So, you can pray for the trial or hardship to end while also praying that God would reveal himself to your brother or sister in a way that will change him or her long after the trial is over.

5. The Public Hurdle. If you're already embracing the concept and practice of deep prayer, then a scary thought may have attacked your mind: Am I supposed to pray like this in public? The answer is No. And Yes. Let's start with

---

[32] Thomas Brooks, *Precious Remedies Against Satan's Devices* (Brookfield, WI: First Rate Publishers, 2013), 42, Apple Books.

The Language of Deep Prayer

the yes.

Both Psalm 74 and Psalm 44 were public prayers of lament. In fact, part of Psalm 44 is a responsive prayer of lament, meaning that the congregation joined in.[33] Laments like these are prayed in public when a public trauma or trial gives rise to the lament. In these two psalms, they were praying about a very public defeat in battle that affected everyone's life and relationship with God. In those cases, the public lament is not only appropriate, but necessary. I still remember the public laments we prayed in church the Sunday following the 9/11 attacks. Public laments could also be prayed when a community is rocked by an earthquake, flood, tornado, or violent crime. When hardship like that hits, the open and authentic emotions of lament belong to the whole community, not just the person praying.

On the other hand, the prayers of Jesus, Job, and Psalm 88 were all private. The relationship you have with God is *your* relationship, not the whole church's, and you should keep that part of it private, including the details of the sin you're confessing and some of your personal opinions about things. In fact, this is what private prayers are for; this is why Jesus told us to go into our rooms, shut the door, and talk to

---

[33]In verses 4 and 6, the cases are singular; in verses 5 and 7-8, the cases are plural. So the worship leader would say, "You are *my* King, O God; ordain salvation for Jacob!" (v. 4) and the congregation would respond, "Through you *we* push down *our* foes; through your name *we* tread down those who rise up against *us*" (v. 5). *See*, Motyer, 116.

DEEP PRAYER

God out of the hearing of others (Matthew 6:6). You cannot grow a deep relationship with God if you only pray in public.

The goal of this chapter was to teach you the language of deep prayer and encourage you to use it. I could tell you that I'm doing this simply because this is the language the Bible teaches us to use, but there is more to it than that. I'm encouraging you to pray this way because, when you talk to God honestly, sincerely, and authentically, you open your soul up to a deeper relationship with the Father, the Son, and the Holy Spirit and, in that openness, God pulls you closer to himself. The great blessing of deep prayer is that it deepens your relationship with God and this deeper relationship changes you, strengthens you, and prepares you to face every challenge, trial, and blessing in your life. How this works is the lesson of the next chapter.

Chapter 5

The Blessing of Deep Prayer

It is impossible to be in a relationship with God and not be changed.

Impossible.

The blessing of deep prayer is a deeper relationship with God; and the blessing of a deeper relationship with God is deep change in your soul.

Jesus had a deeper relationship with his Father than any human being who has ever lived. As both fully God and fully man, he carried in his soul an eternal, spiritual, mutually indwelling relationship with his Father. The supernatural depth of that relationship made every prayer he prayed deeper than any prayer we will ever pray. But then, in Gethsemane, Jesus was confronted with the unthinkable, the impossible, the unbearable prospect of being separated from his Father while he hanged from the cross and died for human sin. Facing this horrible, but inevitable, experience, he confessed to Peter, James, and John, "My soul is sorrowful, even to death." Then he stepped aside to be alone, fell on his face in the dirt, and prayed his deepest prayer (Matthew 26:38-39).

We have focused on the prayer itself: the circumstances leading to it, the horror that produced it, and the words Jesus used in it. But that's not the whole story. The next part of the story is what happened to Jesus because of it. Jesus threw himself down in grief, sadness, and sorrow, but then stood up with the boldness, strength, and courage to face the tidal wave of agony that was about to hit him. During his deep prayer, he connected his soul deeply with his Father and the Father got him ready to go to the cross.

When Jesus finished praying for the third time that night, the mob immediately showed up to arrest Jesus. Instead of shrinking back in pain, Jesus looked his vile betrayer, Judas, in the eye and told him, "Friend, do what you came to do" (Matthew 26:50). Then, when one of his followers pulled out a sword to fight back, Jesus rebuked him: "Put your sword back in its place," and explained, "Do you think that I cannot appeal to my Father, and he will at once send me more than twelve legions of angels? But how then should the Scriptures be fulfilled, that it must be so?" (vv. 52-54). When Jesus had finished praying, he committed himself to following the Father's plan, not his own pain, and this was the first test. Jesus knew he could call on his Father and be rescued by angels, but instead chose to take the path foretold by the prophets: the path of arrest, humiliation, and death.

The Blessing of Deep Prayer

Despite the weakness he felt before his prayer, Jesus had the strength and courage, after his prayer, to submit to this arrest.

Then the mob brought Jesus to the counsel of scribes, elders, and chief priests who had gathered that night to end Jesus's troubling ministry by putting him to death. The high priest, Caiaphas, who was presiding over this council, had an agenda. Before Jesus was arrested, he had told the Jewish leaders that "it was better for you that one man should die for the people, not that the whole nation should perish" (John 11:50). Caiaphas was on a noble mission! He had a higher purpose! He was seeking the greater good! He would put Jesus to death to save the nation of Israel!

So, the tribunal Jesus faced wasn't looking for truth or facts or evidence; they weren't trying to understand what Jesus was doing or teaching; and they certainly weren't administering justice. They were looking for an excuse that they could carry to the Romans that would force the Romans to kill Jesus: "Now the chief priests and the whole council were seeking false testimony against Jesus that they might put him to death, but they found none, though many false witnesses came forward" (Matthew 26:59-60). They were putting on a show of legality in order to break the law.

During Jesus's ministry, he often talked to priests, scribes, elders, and other Jewish leaders. Every time he was confronted by these men, Jesus easily talked circles around them until they were confused or cowed or held in awe by his words. Even now, as they arrested him and dragged him before this bogus tribunal, they still had no clear idea of how to take him down. If Jesus had wanted to avoid the cross, he could have easily exposed this proceeding for the farce that it was and just walked away. Instead, "Jesus remained silent" (v. 63). He let the false witnesses go unchallenged and he let his enemies control the narrative. Later, when his silence would become evidence of his guilt, he said the words that would guarantee his conviction: "But I tell you, from now on you will see the Son of Man seated at the right hand of Power and coming on the clouds of heaven" (v. 64). Everything about this kangaroo court screamed trap, Jesus could see the trap, and he willingly walked right into the trap.

Once they had their bogus conviction, they bound Jesus and delivered him over to Pilate, the Roman governor, so he could finish the job and put Jesus to death (Matthew 27:1-2). Pilate hated the Jews and would have used any excuse available to him to release Jesus, not out of a deep concern for Roman justice but just to stick it to the Jewish leaders. Jesus certainly knew that but, rather than exploiting Pilate's hatred, he kept his mouth shut when Pilate questioned him: "But he gave him no answer, not even to a single charge, so that the governor was greatly amazed" (v. 14).

From the moment Jesus finished praying through his grief over his impending separation from his Father, he walked straight ahead, without hesitation, without weakness, without wavering, to the very cross that would separate him

The Blessing of Deep Prayer

from his Father. He submitted to being beaten, mocked, spit upon, and flogged; he endured being forced to carry his cross until he was too weak from his abuse to carry it further. They stripped him naked, pushed him down on the cross, hammered his hands and feet into place, and then raised him up to endure the worst torture ever seen on this earth—the wrath of his Father poured out on him as he cried out, "My God, my God, why have you forsaken me?" (Matthew 27:46). If Matthew, Mark, and Luke had not recorded Jesus's prayer in Gethsemane, nothing in the way he handled himself from his arrest right up to the tomb would have given us the slightest hint that he had once felt sorrowful to the point of death at any time after the supper or that, because he felt that way, he had asked his Father to change the eternal plan of salvation.

What accounts for such a dramatic change in Jesus in such a short time? The blessing of deep prayer. The deep relationship Jesus had with his Father made it possible for him to pray a deep prayer of honesty, openness, sincerity, and frankness and his deep prayer drew him close to his Father in the moment he felt the pain of their coming separation.

Since Jesus's prayer in Gethsemane is our model for deep prayer, the same blessing is given to us. Through the gospel, through Jesus's death on the cross, we have been given a real relationship with the Triune God, a relationship

God himself describes in the most intimate terms: the Father adopts, the Son betroths, and the Spirit indwells. Inside this wonderful relationship, we can talk to him openly and honestly, sharing our thoughts, our ideas, our sins, our weaknesses, our joys, our pain, our gratitude, and our needs with him at any time in whatever words we can find. As we pray deep prayers we deepen our relationship with God, and that relationship changes us down to the core of our souls. Then, as God changes us, we're able to walk down whatever path he lays out before us. The blessing of deep prayer isn't that God gives us whatever we ask for, it's that God gives us himself—a deeper relationship with our Father and husband through the indwelling Spirit. And that connection with God changes us on the inside, fixing things in our souls we didn't even know were broken. He then pours amazing blessings into us that empowers us to face anything. When we cannot pray deeply, we close our souls off from that deeper relationship and we don't have the strength, grace, or faith to walk boldly into whatever trouble lies ahead. We need to pray deeply for our soul's sake.

Objection: God Can Work without Our Cooperation

Wait just a minute (you might be thinking), God is all-powerful and all-knowing and, if he wants to work on my soul and deepen my relationship with him, he can do whatever he wants, no matter how I pray to him or what I ask him for. That's a good point and, I have to admit, you're absolutely right. God can work on our soul even without our full cooperation.

Consider the apostle Paul, back when he was called Saul and was the enemy of the church. One day, he was making his way from Jerusalem to Damascus with a heart so full of zeal for Judaism that, as soon as he got there, he would start persecuting Christians (Acts 9:1-2). Suddenly, Jesus showed up on the road, blinded him with a bright light, and rebuked him for his foolishness (vv. 3-6). Three days later, God sent Ananias to restore his sight (vv. 9-18) and then, from that day forward, he started preaching the gospel he had once tried to destroy (Galatians 1:23). He considered Jesus dangerous, but Jesus saved him; he was believing a bunch of lies, but Jesus revealed the truth to him; he wanted to stamp out Christianity, but Jesus used him greatly to build up his church.

So, yes, God can work in our souls even if we don't pray the deep prayers that pursue a relationship with him. However, Paul's experience is not the normal way God works in our lives. Even Paul understood that. In Romans 10, as he explained that justification by faith was the same for both Jews and Greeks, he wrote, "For everyone who calls on the name of the Lord will be saved" (v. 13). Right after that, Paul laid out what normally has to happen before someone can call on the name of the Lord and be saved. He didn't mention bright lights or voices from heaven, either.

He laid out a series of secondary causes that God typically uses to get a person to that point:

> How then will they call on him in whom they have not believed? And how are they to believe in him of whom they have never heard? And how are they to hear without someone preaching? And how are they to preach unless they are sent? As it is written, "How beautiful are the feet of those who preach the good news!" (vv. 14-15).

Unbelievers can only be saved by calling on the name of the Lord and they can only call on his name if they believe the gospel and they cannot believe the gospel unless they hear the gospel and they will only hear the gospel if a preacher comes to proclaim it and the preacher will never show up unless a church sends him out. A church cannot sit by, doing nothing, and just wait for God to confront sinners on the road in the miraculous way he confronted Paul. They have to raise money, find a preacher, and send him out to preach. Of course, these are just a representative sample of the various means God uses to work in a person's life, not an exhaustive list. In the first verse of Romans 10, Paul mentioned another important one: "Brothers, my heart's desire and *prayer to God* for them is that they may be saved."

So, while the objection that God can work without our cooperation is true, God himself, in his Word, has made it clear that it's not normal and we shouldn't expect him to work that way. Not only that, but we don't live that way in any other area of our lives. We don't expect God to drop a pile of money into our laps so we can pay our rent or mortgage, we go out and get a job to earn money so we can pay the bills. Instead of expecting God to fill our children's heads with knowledge, we teach them, at home or in school, the things they need to know. Even when we pray the simple prayer, "give us this day our daily bread," we don't expect God to make a loaf of bread appear in our pantry. Instead, he uses a vast array of secondary causes, from the farmer who plants, cultivates, and harvests the wheat, to the miller who buys the wheat and grinds it into flour, to the baker who buys the flour (along with other ingredients) to make the dough, to the oven used to bake the bread, to the truck that carries it to the store, to the store itself that sells the bread, to the way we earn the money to buy it. We expect God to be involved in all those steps, but we never expect him to skip them. He *could* skip them all, like Jesus did when he fed the five thousand, but when he does, we call it a miracle, not the normal.

So, yes, God can do a miracle in your soul without your cooperation, but we should still use every means at our disposal to deepen our relationship with God and experience all the blessings that come with it. When J. C. Ryle wrote *A Call to Prayer* about 150 years ago, he reminded his people that God works in their souls through prayer:

DEEP PRAYER

Nothing is more common than to hear believers complaining that they do not grow in their faith. They tell us that they do not grow in grace, as they would desire. Is it not rather to be suspected that many have just as much grace as they ask for? Is it not true of many, that they have little, because they ask little? The cause of their weakness is to be found in their own stunted, dwarfish, clipped, contracted, hurried, little, narrow, diminutive prayers. *They do not have because they do not ask* [quoting James 4:2]. Oh, reader, we are not limited in Christ, but in ourselves.[34]

We need to pray—not stunted, dwarfish, clipped, contracted, hurried, little, narrow, diminutive prayers—but deep prayers: honest, candid, sincere, vulnerable, frank, bold, authentic, open prayers. Yes, God could (and sometimes does) work in our souls even when we cannot or do not pray deep prayers, but he normally works through these prayers. And he has a really good reason: God isn't an impersonal power that descends on needy souls; God is a person who saved us to have a relationship with us. By responding to our prayers, he encourages us to use the means he created that will deepen our relationship with him. So,

---

[34] I have an old copy of this book, given to me by a former pastor of mine who collected old books. It doesn't have a publication date so I don't know how old it is. It's been reprinted many times since then, however, and is available from several publishers. The content of this book is also included as a chapter in a compilation of Ryle's writings called, *Practical Religion* (Auburn, MA, Evangelical Press, 2001). The quote above is from page 78 of that book.

The Blessing of Deep Prayer

when we pray deep prayers to God, we connect our souls to him and then he changes us on the inside. When we're unwilling to pray deeply to God, we hold him at arm's length and lose the blessing of deep prayer. Now, he will never leave us nor forsake us; he will continue to work in our souls to get us ready for the deeper work; he may even go to work before we're ready; but he normally works through the secondary causes he himself has put in place, and deep prayer is an essential one. If you ignore God's means of opening your soul up to a deeper relationship with him—choosing, perhaps, to wait for an extraordinary work of God—you may be in for a very long wait. We're much better off using what God has provided: the deep prayers that prepare our soul for his deepest work.

The Purpose of Prayer

When, as a foolish teenager, I first became a Christian, I thought that the purpose of prayer was to get answers from a stingy God, to pry open the closed fist that held tightly on to heaven's blessings. I read every book about prayer I could get my hands on because I was fascinated with the idea of using prayer to get God to work for me, to do things in my life that I couldn't do, and to open doors I needed opened. I approached prayer back then a lot like Aladdin approached his genie, except that Aladdin's genie only granted three wishes and my God commanded me to pray without ceasing!

You could say that this idea about God and prayer was

wrong, but that would be far too kind. This idea is borderline blasphemous (and may have even slipped across the border in a couple of places). It's bad, not because I expected way too much from God, but because I wanted so little from him. The kind of prayers I prayed, and the kind of requests you typically hear in corporate prayer meetings at the local church of any denomination—like restored health, a better job, more money, some kind of power or influence, a husband (or a wife), children (or grandchildren), a new house, a better car, getting accepted into the right college, and success in school or vocation—are all so easy for God to do. The God who created the world in six days just by speaking could give anyone these things and more as a gift without lifting a finger. What I didn't understand is that God's goal wasn't to give me stuff, it was to give me a deeper and deeper relationship with himself. As I look back on my prayer life, I have observed something truly amazing: God has answered my prayer when giving me what I asked for would pull me closer to him; and God has not answered my prayers when refusing my request would pull me closer to him. To God, it's never about the stuff we ask him for; it's always about the relationship.

Once I learned that the purpose of prayer is to deepen my relationship with God, then I started to see in the Scriptures the importance of using the language of openness, honesty, authenticity, and sincerity when I prayed. Honesty grows relationships, shows that we trust God with our greatest burdens, deepens the intimacy of our connection, and gives us more of God. And God is the greatest gift God has to give because the closer we get to God, the more we are conformed to the image of Jesus (Romans 8:29), are set free from sin (Romans 6:5-7), and produce the fruit of the Spirit (Galatians 5:16-24).

Keep Praying for Stuff

You might be thinking that, if the purpose of prayer is to deepen your relationship with God, then maybe you should focus all your prayers on growing that relationship. That sounds wise and spiritual, but it's completely wrong. You cannot grow a relationship by talking exclusively about your relationship; you grow a relationship by sharing yourself with the other person as you live among the twists, turns, and turmoil of real life.

Instead of limiting your requests to your relationship with God, you should pray about everything and anything: whatever makes you happy or sad or grateful or frustrated; for small insignificant things and for big, impossible things; for things you really need and for stuff you merely want; for things you think might be God's will for you and for things you're sure are not.[35] Deep prayers are not relational because all you talk about is your relationship with God; deep prayers are relational because, inside your relationship with God, you talk to him about everything that's on your mind or burdening your soul.

Reevaluating Unanswered Prayers

Of course, if you pray like this, you will end up with a very long list of unanswered requests in your prayer journal. I know from long and varied experience that having unanswered prayers can be stressful and cause us to have doubts and fears and may even cause us to back away from God. If you feel this way about unanswered prayers, it's probably because you feel God's love and approval when he answers your prayers—and you feel ignored and rejected when he doesn't. But, once we understand that God uses our prayers, all our prayers—even our unanswered prayers—to deepen our relationship with him, we can evaluate our unanswered prayers very differently. Rather than thinking in terms of "Yes" and "No," we should look to see how our prayers, both the answered and the unanswered, have deepened our relationship with God. To show you what I

---

[35]David prayed that his child by Bathsheba would live after God sent the prophet Nathan to tell him the child would die; Jesus prayed to avoid the cross even though he had volunteered to go to the cross before the world was even created.

The Blessing of Deep Prayer

mean, I have listed four unanswered prayers from the Bible below and, for each one, I consider what God gave to each person while he was saying "No" to their requests.

1. Jesus in Gethsemane. Jesus asked his Father to let him avoid the cross but the Father said no to him, and Jesus went to the cross. He did not receive the thing he asked for, so his prayer went unanswered. But now consider what Jesus did receive through his prayer. He connected his grieving soul to his Father; his Father walked with him down the path toward the cross; and that presence gave him the strength, courage, and determination to do the will of his Father and die alone on the cross while the wrath of his Father poured down on him. On top of that, because Jesus went to the cross, that is, because the Father didn't answer Jesus's prayer, "God has highly exalted him and bestowed on him the name that is above every name, so that at the name of Jesus every knee should bow, in heaven and on earth and under the earth, and every tongue confess that Jesus Christ is Lord, to the glory of God the Father" (Philippians 2:9-11).[36] Jesus didn't get what he asked for but, through his deep prayer, he received much more.

2. David's Prayer for his Son's Life. After King David committed adultery with Bathsheba, got her pregnant, tried to cover up his sin by arranging for her husband to be killed

---

[36]We will look at the connection between Jesus's exaltation and his unanswered prayer in the garden more closely in chapter 7.

in battle so he could marry her, God sent Nathan the prophet to him to tell him God had seen it all and that, as punishment for his sin, his child would die (2 Samuel 12:1, 14). When the baby got sick, David spent a week fasting and praying for the child's life. On the seventh day, the child died. God did not give to David what David asked him for.

But, as we saw in chapter 1, David prayed deep prayers for his son's life (like Psalm 51). So, let's consider what David received because he prayed deeply. First, David experienced forgiveness for his sins. Deep prayer is relational prayer and Psalm 51 shows us that David was seeking to restore the relationship with God that his sin had broken. Before David started praying, Nathan had told him, "The Lord also has put away your sin; you shall not die" (2 Samuel 12:13), so David knew that God had forgiven him. David also knew that his sin had created a distance in that relationship, and he sought after God to restore the closeness they once had with each other. Second, God gave David another son, conceived inside his marriage with Bathsheba. David had lots of sons, but this one was Solomon, the son who was given great wisdom by God, who inherited the throne from his father, who expanded the kingdom David left him, and who would fulfill his father's plans by building God's temple in Jerusalem. Yes, David lost his son but, inside his restored relationship with God, David received greater blessings than he even asked for.

3. Job's Prayers. Job's first prayer in his trial (in chapter

The Blessing of Deep Prayer

3) was a deep lament that attempted to give words to the intensity of his suffering and pain. Job cried out that he wished he had never been born or, if he had to be born, he wished he would have died immediately after the delivery. When I read this passage, it sounds like Job is complaining about his trial, not asking God for anything. After all, Job was born and he had lived to see his trial; he cannot be asking God to undo what has been done. And, while that's true, it turns out it was more than that to Job. As Job continued to pray in his trial, he kept asking for the same thing—not to go back in time and keep him from being born, but to end his life right now. At one point, he told his friends, "Oh that I might have my request, and that God would fulfill my hope, that it would please God to crush me, that he would let loose his hand and cut me off!" (Job 6:8-9). A little while later, Job directed this same request to God:

> I loathe my life; I would not live forever.
> > Leave me alone, for my days are a breath.
> What is man, that you make so much of him,
> > and that you set your heart on him,
> visit him every morning
> > and test him every moment?
> How long will you not look away from me,
> > nor leave me alone till I swallow my spit?
> (Job 7:16-19).

In chapter 10, Job prays for this again. He starts this prayer by crying out, "I loathe my life; I will give free utterance to my complaint; I will speak in the bitterness of my soul" (Job 10:1). Then he repeats his prayer from chapter 3—"Why did you bring me out of the womb?"—and connects it to his current request to go to the grave in peace:

> Why did you bring me out from the womb?
> > Would that I had died before any eye had seen me
> and were as though I had not been,
> > carried from the womb to the grave.
> Are not my days few?
> Then cease, and leave me alone, that I may find a little cheer
> > before I go—and I shall not return—
> > > to the land of darkness and deep shadow,
> > the land of gloom like thick darkness,
> > > like deep shadow without any order,
> > > where light is as thick darkness
> > (Job 10:18-22).

God refused Job's repeated requests for death to come to him. Instead, God gave him something far, far better. Starting in chapter 38, God finally spoke to Job, revealing himself to him. He showed Job his wisdom—greater wisdom than Job could ever imagine. He showed Job his power—the great power that created and governs the universe. He never told Job why he suffered, but he did teach Job a lot about the way God works in the lives of men. Job was closer to God at the end of his trial, and he knew God more intimately because of his trial, which is the greatest gift God can give. Here is how Job reacted after God spoke and revealed himself to Job: "I had heard of you by the hearing of the ear, but now my eye sees you; therefore I despise myself, and repent in dust and ashes" (Job 42:5-6).

Job acknowledged that, before God spoke, his understanding was weaker (described as merely hearing about God) but, after God spoke, his understanding became much greater, much deeper (described as seeing God with his eye). Not only that, but once Job had this clearer revelation of God, he also had a clearer revelation of himself. Looking back at all that Job had said to God, he realized how much of it was stupid, so he repented. Throughout the entire book, Job refused to repent of any sin, despite the constant urgings of his friends, but when God revealed himself more fully to him, Job repented for thinking he knew God and had been close with God. That's the blessing of deep prayer: A relationship with God so much deeper that the old relationship seems like nothing in comparison.

4. Paul's Prayer for his Thorn. Paul was given massive revelations by God, including visions, dreams, and some kind of experience of being in the third heaven, in the immediate presence of God himself. But these great revelations came with a danger: Paul could easily become conceited. So, Paul told the Corinthians, "to keep me from becoming conceited because of the surpassing greatness of the revelations, a thorn was given me in the flesh, a messenger of Satan to harass me, to keep me from becoming conceited" (2 Corinthians 12:7). Unsurprisingly, Paul didn't like having a thorn in his flesh so, "Three times I pleaded with the Lord about this, that it should leave me" (v. 8). But Paul's prayer was not answered. He had to live with this thorn, presumably for the rest of his life.

Paul himself tells us what God gave him through his deep prayers for the removal of his thorn:

> "But [God] said to me, 'My grace is sufficient for you, for my power is made perfect in weakness.' Therefore I will boast all the more gladly of my weaknesses, so that the power of Christ my rest upon me. For the sake of Christ, then, I am content with weaknesses, insults, hardships, persecutions, and calamities. For when I am weak, then I am strong" (vv. 9-10).

Paul received more of God himself. The presence of God in his life included God's amazing grace to bear the burden of the thorn and God's incredible power to offset the weakness that the thorn created. But there is even more than that. Since the thorn was given to Paul to prevent conceit over the revelations God was giving him, it's possible that the removal of the thorn would have meant removing all future revelation. When Paul got more of God, in the form of his grace and strength, Paul also continued to receive these great revelations from God. Paul got far more blessings from having his prayers unanswered than he would have by having his thorn removed.

The Blessing of Deep Prayer

Deep Prayer is Not a Gimmick

As I told you, I spent a lot of time studying prayer in an attempt to discover the "secret key" that would unlock heaven's blessing, so I need to make sure you're not doing the same thing as you read this book. Deep prayer is not a gimmick. Deep prayer will connect you to your Father in heaven who will pour amazing blessings into your life, but those prayers do not make your life easier, they make your soul stronger; they don't always get you what you ask for, but they get you what you need; they don't always change your circumstances, but they always change you.

When Jesus prayed in the garden that night, his prayers didn't turn the whips the Romans used on his back into long strands of overcooked spaghetti, or transform the thorns on the crown they jammed into his scull into soft foam, or change the wood of the cross he was forced to carry into light cork, or digitize the nails they drove into his body into a painless hologram, or make hanging on the cross feel like he was lying in a comfy bed.

And yet, because he connected his soul to his Father through his deep prayer, the same Jesus who was a quivering pile of sweat and tears in the garden was a towering pillar of strength and purpose everywhere else. Even though he asked his Father to let him avoid the hardship, his prayer gave him the strength to live through the hardship instead.

Deep prayers to be healed of your cancer may not remove the cancer, but God will use that prayer to give you the grace to live with it, the power to minister to others because of it, and the ability to rejoice in the time you have left on this earth. Deep prayers asking God to give you more money may not increase your wealth, but God will use that prayer to empower you to manage what you have more faithfully, increase your gratitude to God for his provision, and grow your contentment with your circumstances. Deep prayers that tell God how much you hate being single and desperately need to get married may not bring a spouse to you, but God will use that prayer to give you more grace to live alone, to provide opportunities that you would have missed if you were married, and to open your eyes to the blessings right in front of you.

We pray deep prayers not to manipulate God into giving us his lesser blessings, but to consistently receive his greatest blessing: a closer relationship with him. Inside that growing relationship God will give us what we need most.

The Blessing of *Answered* Prayer

Before we end this chapter, I want to make sure I don't leave you with the impression that God doesn't answer prayers or, that when he does, it's not that big of a deal. Our Father does answer his beloved children and, when he does, it's often "far more abundantly than all that we ask or think" (Ephesians 3:20). But the lesson of this chapter is that, even

The Blessing of Deep Prayer

when he gives us exactly what we ask for, the deepening of the relationship is still his greatest blessing. Here are two examples from my own experience.

There was a time in my life when I was seriously underemployed for about 10 years. Across that decade, I cried out to God for direction, for wisdom, and just for a job. This was the agonizing trial in which I learned to speak the language of deep prayer. With each passing year, God pulled me closer and closer to himself, deepened my understanding of his Word, and showed me the beauty of his character. Then, one day, he opened a huge door and gave me the exact kind of job I had been asking for, with challenging work, excellent co-workers, and a very good salary package. It was the kind of job that changed the trajectory of my life and set my feet on solid ground again. All the prayers I had cried out to God were answered in wonderful detail. However, as wonderful as that answered prayer has been, the greater blessing was the 10 years of unanswered prayers that brought me closer to him.

When my youngest son went off to war, my wife began to pray earnestly for him. She started by praying for what she wanted most: his safe return. But as she prayed, her prayers became more and more specific about his daily life and the missions he went on. She asked God to give his leaders the courage to protect his unit from those above them who might consider their lives expendable. She asked God to protect the

DEEP PRAYER

men on his team and that they would watch each other's back. She even asked God to cause the enemy to fear them, so much so that they would refuse to engage them as they moved through their region.

When my son made it safely home and started telling us about his experiences, we were amazed to see that my wife's prayers had been answered down to the smallest detail. In fact, not one person in his entire battalion died on this deployment, a first in the war up to that point. God had intervened in the global war on terror to answer my wife's specific prayers. I'm sure you can imagine how excited and grateful we were as this reality unfolded for us. But what was just as amazing to us was that, as my wife prayed over those seven months, she was as close to God as she had ever been. It was so intimate and special that she began to realize that she wasn't merely praying these prayers, but God himself was giving her the prayers to pray. She was hanging out with God each day and, as she talked to God, he took part in the conversation and led her to pray according to his will and plan, both for global events and for family concerns.

CHAPTER 6
THE CONVERSATION OF DEEP PRAYER

Have you ever known someone who talks too much? Someone who, no matter what situation he is in, dominates the conversation by talking so much about himself—his interests, his problems, his feelings, his opinions—that you can never get a word in? How would you describe your relationship with a person like that? It seems like you're friends; after all, you certainly know a lot about him. The problem is that he doesn't know you at all. As he keeps talking and talking and talking, he shows a great interest in himself, but shows very little interest in you: getting to know you, learning your opinions on whatever he is babbling on about, or understanding how his thoughts compare with yours. Whatever this relationship is, it is certainly not a deep friendship.

Now here is the bad news: in your relationship with God, there is a danger that you can become the person who does all the talking and never listens. And yes, I am aware that I have spent the entire book up to this point encouraging you to talk to God—to tell him everything that's on your mind, to tell him what you feel, to tell him what you want, to talk and talk and talk to him as much as you can. But I have also emphasized that deep prayer is relational prayer and I even defined prayer as a *conversation* with God, not just as talking to God. To forge a deep relationship with God, you not only have to talk to him openly and authentically, but you also have to listen to him honestly and courageously.

How to Listen to God

When I was a baby Christian, people who had been in Christ for many years encouraged me to start doing two things right away: first, pray to God; second, read the Bible. They urged me to make this a regular habit of my life—actually a regular habit of each day! I didn't realize it at the time, but I was being taught, right from the start, to have a conversation with God.

God speaks to us through the Bible. The book of Hebrews starts off by telling us that the Bible exists because God spoke: "Long ago, at many times and in many ways, God spoke to our fathers by the prophets, but in these last days he has spoken to us by his Son, whom he appointed the heir of all things, through whom also he created the world" (Hebrews 1:1-2). The Old Testament is the written record of what God spoke to the Jewish people through the prophets. The New Testament is the written record of what God spoke to the Christian church through his Son. Both these Testaments have been given to us by the Holy Spirit so that we can hear God speak to us. The Bible, then, is God's side of the conversation.

The Conversation of Deep Prayer

Yes, the prophets who wrote the Old Testament were human beings and Jesus's disciples who wrote the New Testament were human beings, but Peter made it clear that it is still God who speaks, explaining that "no prophecy of Scripture comes from someone's own interpretation. For no prophecy was ever produced by the will of man, but *men spoke from God as they were carried along by the Holy Spirit*" (1 Peter 1:20-21). Paul wrote the same thing to his disciple, Timothy: "*All Scripture is breathed out by God* and profitable for teaching, for reproof, for correction, and for training in righteousness, that the man of God may be complete, equipped for every good work" (2 Timothy 3:16-17). So, whenever we open the Bible and start to read, we are listening to God himself speak to us. As B. B. Warfield explained, "What Scripture says, God says."[37]

We can listen to God speak to us anytime we want simply by opening the Bible and reading his Words. Most Christians today have their own Bible, along with access to every kind of help they need to understand it. We just need to read it. In my opening illustration, the talkative man never gets to know you because he will not let you speak. But God is constantly speaking through the Bible so, if you don't know him, it's because you will not listen to what he has

---

[37]Benjamin Breckinridge Warfield, *The Inspiration and Authority of the Bible* (Phillipsburg, NJ, The Presbyterian and Reformed Publishing Company, 1948), 145.

already said. You cannot have a deep relationship with God unless you get to know him; and you cannot get to know God unless you listen to his side of the conversation; and you cannot listen to God's side of the conversation unless you take in the message of the Bible regularly, systematically, and seriously.

I know that the Bible is a long and complicated book. Just thinking about reading it can be intimidating. But you do not have to read the whole book in a couple of days, you just have to start reading it.[38] I suggest you focus on the New Testament without neglecting the Old Testament but find a plan that will keep you reading through it. Our world gives us lots of distractions that can keep us from sitting quietly and reading the Bible, everything from "I work twelve hours a day" or "The kids were throwing up all night" to "I don't like to read" or "My Instagram account isn't going to update itself." All I can say to this is that listening to God is supremely important. Find a way to do it inside the serious things you have to do in your life and make it a higher priority than the frivolous things you want to do in your life.

---

[38]There are many good and helpful guides to the Bible that can teach you how it is laid out, the different kinds of literature that are used, and some of the history that the books are set in. They will also give you a short introduction to each book that can help you hear the message more easily. Just remember, these are tools to help you understand what you're reading. The goal is to read.

The Conversation of Deep Prayer

It will be hard at first but, if you keep with it, I promise you it will be worth the effort.

A second way you can take in the message of the Bible and listen to God is by attending a church that preaches and teaches the Bible. The method of preaching and teaching that best presents the meaning and message of the Bible is called "expository." That just means the preacher pulls the original meaning out of a passage, shapes the sermon or lesson around it, and presents it to the people. An expository sermon will not only help you hear what God is saying to you in the passage being preached, but listening to these kinds of sermons week after week will also help you when you're reading other parts of the Bible on your own.

As you read, and even study, the Bible, just keep in mind what you're doing. You're listening to God as he tells you about himself; you're listening to God's side of your conversation of deep prayer. Don't make the mistake I made when I started reading. I treated the Bible as a body of information to be learned and then mastered, as a source of correct doctrine and objective truth. Now, the Bible is our only authoritative source of correct doctrine and it is filled with objective truth, but those wonderful things serve an even more wonderful purpose: they all reveal the living God to us—Father and Son and Holy Spirit—so we can know him and love him; so we can talk to him and listen to him; so we can have a deep relationship with him that changes us down to the core of our souls.

DEEP PRAYER

As I mentioned earlier, deep relationships like this are not created in a moment, they develop over a long time; we don't get to know anyone—much less the infinite God—in an instant. We get to know others step by step over time. However, you don't have to know everything about a person to be blessed by and enjoy the relationship you're in. On your very first day as a Christian, you can be blessed by listening to God and talking to him in deep prayer; but then, after 50 years, you can be blessed by how much more you have learned about the unfathomable nature, person, work, and beauty of the Father who has adopted you, the Son who has betrothed you, and the Spirit who indwells you.

Case Study: Habakkuk's Conversation with God

What does this conversation look like? God recorded a conversation he had with a prophet named Habakkuk that shows us just how he engages us through our deep prayers. Habakkuk lived in the southern kingdom of Judah after the northern kingdom of Israel had been conquered by Assyria, but before the Babylonians attacked and destroyed Jerusalem. The whole book is laid out as a conversation between Habakkuk and God, starting with Habakkuk's deep prayer about the moral depravity of the people living around him. God then speaks to Habakkuk and the rest of the book shows us the back-and-forth conversation between God and his prophet. As the conversation moves forward, Habakkuk comes to understand God more deeply and Habakkuk's heart

The Conversation of Deep Prayer

changes until he is able to embrace the plan God had revealed to him.

Habakkuk's first prayer was a deep prayer of complaint to God about the sin he saw all around him and his desire for God to deal with it:

> O LORD, how long shall I cry for help,
>   and you will not hear?
> Or cry to you "Violence!"
>   and you will not save?
> Why do you make me see iniquity,
>   and why do you idly look at wrong?
> Destruction and violence are before me;
>   strife and contention arise.
> So the law is paralyzed,
>   and justice never goes forth.
> For the wicked surround the righteous;
>   so justice goes forth perverted
>   (Habakkuk 1:2-4).

Everywhere he looked, Habakkuk saw sin. Not just little sins, either, but sins of violence and destruction for which there was never any justice. Habakkuk grieved deeply over these sins, by the rush of God's chosen people to become like every other nation around it, and by God's apparent indifference to it all. Habakkuk wanted God to judge the sinners, purge the sin from the nation, and make Israel holy once again.

Habakkuk was honest and open when he talked to God, but he was also ready to listen when God spoke to him. And, since Habakkuk was a prophet, God spoke directly to him, telling him exactly how he planned to deal with Israel's sins:

> Look among the nations, and see;
>   wonder and be astounded.
> For I am doing a work in your days
>   that you would not believe if told.
> For behold, I am raising up the Chaldeans,
>   that bitter and hasty nation,
> who march through the breadth of the earth,
>   to seize dwellings not their own (vv. 5-6).

This was not the answer Habakkuk was looking for! Habakkuk asked God to come down and deal with the sinners in Israel so Israel could be holy again. Instead, God told him he was calling the dreaded army of the Chaldeans from the kingdom of Babylon to conquer Israel and remove everyone—the sinners and the faithful—from the land. This was shocking enough, but God kept on talking, reciting fact after fact about the cruelty of the Babylonians that would have turned Habakkuk's shock into despair. He reminded Habakkuk of their reputation: "They are dreaded and fearsome" (v. 7). He described, in colorful metaphors, their skill in battle: "Their horses are swifter than leopards, more fierce than the evening wolves; their horsemen press proudly on. Their horsemen come from afar; they fly like an eagle swift to devour" (v. 8). He revealed their motive, too: "They all come for violence, all their faces forward. They gather captives like sand" (v. 9). Just in case Habakkuk was harboring hope that Judah could withstand the onslaught,

The Conversation of Deep Prayer

God told him, "At kings they scoff, and at rulers they laugh. They laugh at every fortress, for they pile up earth and take it" (v. 10). Finally, he reminded Habakkuk of their godlessness: "Then they sweep by like the wind and go on, *guilty men, whose own might is their god!*" (v. 11).

After hearing that pronouncement from God, Habakkuk was no longer concerned about the injustice and sin he had seen throughout Judah; he never complained again that God was looking idly at Israel's wrongdoing. Justice was coming at the hands of the Babylonians, and they would bring more violence and more destruction than Habakkuk wanted to see. So, he had a new complaint, not about Israelite sin or about Babylonian ruthlessness, but about God himself:

> Are you not from eternity,
>   Yahweh my God?
>   My Holy One, You will not die.
> LORD, You appointed them to execute judgment;
>   My Rock, You destined them to punish us.
> Your eyes are too pure to look at evil,
>   and You cannot tolerate wrongdoing.
> So why are You silent
>   while one who is wicked swallows up
>   one who is more righteous than himself?
>   (vv. 12-13, HCSB)

In another brutally honest prayer, Habakkuk questions God's decision to send Babylon to destroy Israel. He starts off with words that sound like praise or, at the least, an acknowledgement of God's character: you are eternal, you are holy, you are my Rock, you are pure. But I think those words really express Habakkuk's total confusion over what he just heard. He confesses the trauma he's feeling at the end of verse 13: How could the holy God judge Israel's sins by using a nation even more sinful than they were? None of this makes sense to him. After all, God is still alive, right? God is still holy, right? So, in his turmoil, Habakkuk calls out to God to ask how he could destroy his own people and how he could use a nation without a single redeemable quality to be an instrument of justice. In verses 14 through 16, Habakkuk compared the world to the fish in the sea and the Babylonians to the fishermen who catch them in their nets, kill them, sell them, live in luxury, and then worship the net that caught the fish. In verse 17, he asked God, "Is he then to keep on emptying his net and mercilessly killing nations forever?"

Do you see how this conversation works? Habakkuk was concerned about the level of sin and violence he saw around him in Israel, so he prayed that God would judge the nation and restore it to righteousness. Then God spoke and told Habakkuk what was coming. What God revealed to him gave Habakkuk some answers, but it also raised a whole new set of questions—questions about how God executes his justice. So, Habakkuk went back to God and prayed another deep prayer, this time expressing his own confusion about God's plan. The entire conversation shifted direction

The Conversation of Deep Prayer

because of what God revealed to Habakkuk when he spoke. Keep this in mind for later because I'm going to show you how God converses with us in the same way through the Bible.

Habakkuk is a short book that we can read quickly, but this conversation between Habakkuk and God was anything but quick. After Habakkuk prayed his second prayer, God didn't answer him right away, and Habakkuk had to wait to hear again from God. He wrote, "I will take my stand at my watchpost and station myself on the tower, and look out to see what he will say to me, and what I will answer concerning my complaint" (2:1). He had to wait for the answer, but he wasn't being passive and aloof while he waited. He was actively waiting, like a watchman on guard over a city looking out for a messenger who is expected but whose schedule is unknown. This is a picture of a man still engaged with God and, presumably, still praying to God while he was waiting.

Eventually, God came to Habakkuk and answered him. His answer showed Habakkuk that God's justice is always at work in the world, although often unseen until it comes to fruition. God reveals this through five "Woe to him" statements explaining that the evil inflicted by Babylon on others will ultimately roll back on the whole empire and destroy it. Look at the first of these pronouncements:

> Shall not all these take up their taunt against him,
>   with scoffing and riddles for him, and say,
>   "Woe to him who heaps up what is not his own—
>   for how long?—
>   and loads himself with pledges!"
> Will not your debtors suddenly arise,
>   and those awake who will make you tremble?
>   Then you will be spoil for them.
> Because you have plundered many nations,
>   all the remnant of the peoples shall plunder you,
>   for the blood of man and violence to the earth,
>   to cities and all who dwell in them
>   (Habakkuk 2:6-8).

The key to the judgement is at the end of verse 7: "Then *you* will be spoil for *them*." All those whom Babylon had plundered would eventually plunder Babylon. Notice that this judgement is already in the works. The discontent and hatred against Babylon is seething and bubbling under the surface in all the people they have conquered and enslaved, just waiting for the spark to set them off.

The first four of these woes follow the same pattern, showing Habakkuk that the wealth, power, and security of Babylon is all a façade that hides the working of God's judgement against them. God is not idly looking at wrong. He is not remaining silent while Babylon swallows up nation after nation. Instead, he is working under the surface, preparing their destruction by bringing back on them the evil they have long inflicted on others.

The Conversation of Deep Prayer

Habakkuk responded to this revelation, just as he had always done, with even deeper prayer. This time his prayer accepted God's plan for both Israel and Babylon and praised God's justice and wrath against sin in the world while asking that in his wrath God remember mercy (Habakkuk 3:2). He fully accepted this plan, even though it was frightening: "I hear, and my body trembles; my lips quiver at the sound; rottenness enters into my bones; my legs tremble beneath me. Yet I will quietly wait for the day of trouble to come upon people who invade us" (Habakkuk 3:16). He also committed himself to trust in God no matter what happened in the future, not merely submitting to the will of God, but actually desiring his will be done here on this earth:

> Though the fig tree should not blossom,
>   nor fruit be on the vines,
> the produce of the olive fail
>   and the fields yield no food,
> the flock be cut off from the fold
>   and there be no herd in the stalls,
> yet I will rejoice in the Lord;
>   I will take joy in the God of my salvation.
> God, the LORD, is my strength;
>   he makes my feet like the deer's;
>   he makes me tread on my high places
>   (vv. 17-19).

A Conversation with God

Whenever we pray deep and honest prayers to God, we open up a conversation with him, like Habakkuk did, a conversation where our prayers signal to God that we're ready to hear what he has to say and that our souls are open to his work; a conversation in which he reveals more and more of himself to us, until we understand a little better who he is and what he is doing. But this cannot be a one-sided conversation, where we do all the talking. After praying deeply, we then have to listen honestly and courageously to what God says.

Honesty and courage are needed because we have to go to the Bible to listen to its words, not to find proof for what we already want to do. God uses his Word to reveal himself to us, but we can only grow closer to God if we're listening to him honestly. Reading honestly means you seek out God's message, listening to both God's encouragements and promises along with his rebukes and warnings.

You also need to read the Bible courageously because, in the Bible, God will expose your sin, sin you weren't even aware of; he will rebuke you for the very things in your life that you're most proud of; he will warn you of dangers you cannot see. For people like us, long trained in avoidance and deflection, courage is needed to hear hard truths. But, if you listen to the Bible honestly, the message you hear will enable you to be honest with yourself, will renew your mind, and will reveal God to you—all of which will transform your soul.

You do not have to be afraid of any of this. If the Bible exposes your sin, fear not! Those sins are forgiven through

The Conversation of Deep Prayer

the sacrifice of Jesus on the cross. The rebukes and warnings are not coming from a judge pronouncing a horrible sentence, they are being spoken by a loving Father correcting wayward children. Even when you read something hard, something you don't want to hear, or are not strong enough to do, you can always run to God in deep prayer and tell him how you feel. When Habakkuk heard God say the Babylonians were coming to judge his country, he didn't like what he heard but, instead of reinterpreting the message to be more palatable, he brought the message back to God and exclaimed, "Are you kidding me?!" Your Father in heaven invites you to do exactly the same thing. When you read something that makes you sad, or rebukes your behavior, or challenges the way you think about the world, or calls you to an action you don't like, don't drop the Bible and stop praying. Listen to the Bible, be honest with yourself, and then be honest with God in prayer. And yes, as we have seen over and over again, that honest prayer can be something like, "I don't want this!" or "I don't understand this!" or "I hate this!" or even "I don't believe this!" Have an honest conversation with your loving Father.

These kinds of conversations take time. I don't mean the time it takes to read a chapter and say a quick prayer, either. They can take weeks, months, even years. I had a conversation with God about how my sorry soul didn't line up with a specific passage in the Bible that lasted a decade!

God knows that our souls need to be brought closer to him in increments, not all at once. If God revealed himself to you all at once, you wouldn't grow, you would die. So, God builds your soul up in one area and that becomes the foundation for showing you something else in another area which then gives you strength to handle another insight which then leads you to seeing God more clearly and praising him for what he has done inside you. These conversations can be long, but they are never boring.

When you first became a Christian, I'm sure you were told to read your Bible and pray to God, just like I was. I hope you listened. However, even among those who have regular quiet times, it can be easy to approach this more like a daily duty than a dynamic conversation. I encourage you to change your approach to both the Bible and prayer. Instead of a duty, instead of a task to check off, think of your quiet time as a dynamic conversation with God, the time when you have a chance to tell your Father everything that's on your mind and heart, and where you can then hear his wisdom and grow closer to him. In these conversations, the intimacy of your relationship will grow, your understanding of God will overwhelm you, your soul will expand immeasurably, you will get stronger and become more faithful. In short, you will love the Lord your God with more and more of your heart, soul, mind, and strength and, inside that relationship, you will find everything you need for life and godliness. You will also find that you have moved from complaining about what God is doing to praising and thanking God for what he has done. Nothing about this will be easy for you, but everything about this is a great blessing to your soul.

It would be nice if, every time we prayed a deep prayer to God, he would speak to us directly and intentionally, like he spoke to Habakkuk. Unfortunately, this kind of clear back-and-forth, give-and-take conversation doesn't always happen. Sometimes we pray and even get an answer, but the answer doesn't stick, and we have to pray the same prayers over and over again. Sometimes, instead of speaking directly to us through his Word, he uses the people around us to poke and prod us while we wait for God to answer. Still other times, he doesn't speak at all, but makes us wait for the answer. All three of these are conversations of deep prayer. To help you recognize and participate in these conversations as you are going through them, the rest of the chapter will show you a biblical example of each one of them. We start (as always) in the Garden of Gethsemane and Jesus's conversation of deep prayer with his Father.

Needing the Same Answer Over and Over Again

Sometimes, when we talk to God about our burden, he not only speaks to us, he gives us the answer we need. Then, as we get up from our prayers, the answer helps us, encourages us, even frees us, but we cannot seem to hold on to that answer. Later, the burden comes back, and we have to talk to our Father again. He then gives us the same answer and that seems to settle things. Until it doesn't, and we have to go back to our Father once again.

This happened to Jesus as he prayed in the garden just before his arrest. I have written about the heavy burden that prompted this prayer, about what Jesus asked for, and about how Jesus got up from this prayer and marched straight to the cross. Now let's consider the flow of the prayer itself. This was a prayer in three parts. In the first part, here is what happened: "And going a little farther he fell on his face and prayed, saying, 'My Father, if it be possible, let this cup pass from me; nevertheless, not as I will, but as you will'" (Matthew 26:39).

As Jesus struggled with his impending separation from his Father—as he talked to and then listened to his Father—Jesus had a breakthrough. The pain that prompted the prayer gave way to submission to his Father. Just imagine the massive release Jesus must have felt when he could say, "nevertheless, not as I will, but as you will." He fell to his face in great pain over the separation he would soon experience on the cross, but his Father encouraged him and strengthened him until Jesus was ready to move ahead with the plan.

Or was he? Jesus went back to Peter, James, and John, found them sleeping, and had to warn them (again) about what was coming. But then he needed to go back to his

The Conversation of Deep Prayer

isolated spot and pray again. But this prayer didn't build on the relief he had just received. Jesus didn't go back to his Father and say, Okay, now that we've got that settled, let's talk out all the details. Instead, he prayed the same thing, "My Father, if this cannot pass unless I drink it . . . ." until he came to the same conclusion: ". . . your will be done" (Matthew 26:42). Once again it looked like Jesus was encouraged and strengthened and ready to move on. But he wasn't. When he went back to his disciples the next time and found them sleeping, he didn't even bother to wake them up; he just walked away from them, found his praying spot, and "prayed for the third time, saying the same words again" (Matthew 26:44).

Jesus kept going back and prayed the same prayer to his Father, even after receiving comfort from his Father. Jesus kept going back to talk to his Father even though he got the answer he needed each time he prayed. I'm sure he would have prayed again, but he ran out of time. After his third prayer, he looked up and saw his betrayer coming with a crowd, ready to arrest him (Matthew 26:45-47).

Why did Jesus keep praying? Because some pain is so deep, so intense, that it doesn't go away even after God speaks to you and you learn something or experience something or make a breakthrough that seemed to confront and defeat the pain. Some pain keeps coming back up over and over again, triggered by hearing a casual comment or listening to a harmless melody or seeing a mundane action or even catching a whiff of a familiar smell. Suddenly, the pain you thought you had worked through and prayed through is back, feeling like it had never left or been resolved.

This kind of thing happens all the time to adults who have suffered abuse as children, whether that abuse is sexual, physical, mental, or emotional. When children face these kinds of horrors, they try to work through them in their own minds, by themselves. Since they are children, what they tell themselves to reconcile their minds and emotions to the way they are being treated may be wildly inaccurate, but these rationalizations still become the lens through which they see the world. Even after coming to Jesus, even after being forgiven of all their sins, even after being adopted into God's family, even after talking through their trauma with others, even after praying to their Father in heaven, childhood memories and that childish worldview will regularly come back to afflict them.

Soldiers who fight a hard battle, killing the enemy and seeing their friends killed, will feel the euphoria of victory immediately after the bullets stop flying, only to see the horrors of the battle in their mind over and over again when they are safe back home. They may be going to church every week and reading the Bible every day, but still, months and even years later, they can hear a car backfire that will bring the feelings of their battles back to them and cause them to

The Conversation of Deep Prayer

look for danger around every corner.

Even the rest of us, Christians who haven't suffered through intense trauma, go through this. As we grew up, we found things that comforted us, gave us pleasure, allowed us to escape the stresses of life, or gave us courage, and we find ourselves going back to those things when we want comfort or pleasure or escape or courage. Those things might be horribly sinful or merely harmful but, whatever they are, we keep getting ensnared by them and have to go back to our Father to talk through it all once again.

God is working in us to free us of all these traumas as we connect to him through deep prayer. So, through the work of Jesus, he forgives all the sins that shaped our souls into its current state of deformity; through his Word, he teaches us the truth, including what's right and what's wrong; through the Holy Spirit, he himself comes to live inside of us. Inside this relationship, he uses all of those past experiences to shape our new lives inside his family. Not in an instant, not in an hour, not after three sessions of prayer; but he keeps moving us all, step by step, toward freedom. As part of that process, he welcomes us back into his presence to pray the same prayers over and over again: confessing the same sins, grieving over the same hurts, expressing the same pain over the same trauma. He is gracious, patient, understanding, and kind to us as we keep going back to him.

When you have to constantly come back to your Father, especially when you've repeated the same prayer for the hundredth time, it's easy to think, "This deep prayer thing didn't work at all; I'm right back where I started from," or to think, "Jesus only had to pray three times to get over his pain and I'm still here years later. What's wrong with me?" That's the wrong lesson to learn. The right lesson is that the Father calls you back to himself to deepen the relationship as you pray that same prayer over and over again as many times as it takes. That's what Jesus did.

Never stop praying deep prayers, even the same deep prayer multiple times, because that's one way we have an ongoing conversation with our God. As time passes, you will live in freedom more and more frequently and for longer stretches of time before the old feelings or habits snap back in your life. It may feel like you're back at square one, but you're not. You're just having those same feelings inside your growing relationship with God, where your soul is getting stronger and your old chains are getting weaker.

Using People to Speak to Us

Job also had a conversation with God. Although God did not speak to Job until chapter 38, Job's conversation with God still had a back-and-forth quality to it, like Habakkuk's conversation in his book. The big difference is that, whenever Job spoke, it wasn't God who responded, it was one of Job's friends. A large section of the book of Job (chapters 4 through 31) centers around the conversation Job had with the three friends who came to comfort Job after he

The Conversation of Deep Prayer

had been afflicted (Job 2:11-13). After Job's deep lament in chapter 3, the book is laid out in a pattern where one of Job's friends speaks to him and Job responds. Then, after all three have spoken (and Job has responded), the pattern repeats two more times.

One of the striking features of the book of Job is how completely wrong his three friends are about everything that had been going on in Job's life. They were wrong about Job, wrong about why Job was suffering, and wrong about how Job should respond to his suffering. And, when they talked about God, they were not always wrong, but they were always foolish (Job 42:7-9). However, these conversations were used by God to force Job to think through his own character, to reconcile his situation with God's character, to reexamine how God works in the world, and to reconsider his relationship with God. These bad counsellors were instruments of God to help Job along the path toward a deeper understanding of God. Job desperately wanted to talk to God,[39] but God used these men to get Job thinking and talking. God engaged Job in a conversation through these men.

God does the same thing to us, conversing with us by bringing people into our lives to force us to think more deeply and seriously about our problems and our sin, to get

---

[39] *See* Job 13:3, 13-22; 23:2-7; 31:35-37.

us to dig deeply into the Bible, to spur us to learn more about God so we can seek him and know him. Some of these people will be like Job's friends: they will come to you with preconceived ideas about God that don't fit your situation, they will refuse to listen to you in your pain, they will tell you God has rejected you, and they will judge you just for being in pain in the first place. As hard as it is to be around people like that, God will still use them to engage you in conversation with the goal of drawing you closer to himself.

Fortunately for all Christians everywhere, God will also bring people into your life who know him well, who are willing to listen to you, who come alongside and bear some of your burdens, who graciously point out sin (not to condemn you but to help you through it), and who share God's true character with you in your troubles. These people will also become part of your conversation with God.

Jesus gave us the church to surround us with people who speak to us on God's behalf and to whom we speak on God's behalf. I know it's easy to think of the other members of our church as just people we have fellowship with, but Paul makes it clear that, when we go to church, we are interacting with others as part of the body of Christ himself.[40] Inside

---

[40] Paul calls the church the body of Christ in four of his letters recorded in the New Testament (all written to local churches): Romans 12:5; 1 Corinthians 12:27 Ephesians 4:11-16; Colossians 2:18-19 and 3:15.

The Conversation of Deep Prayer

this body, we use our gifts to make the body stronger and healthier while the other members of the church use their gifts to help us grow (Ephesians 4:15-16). The people in this church—the weak and the strong, the foolish and the wise, the childish and the mature—are used by God the way God used Job's counsellors. The great difference is that, since the church is the body of Christ, we're interacting with Jesus himself as we interact with the people in our church. Jesus told us that "as you [ministered to] one of the least of these, my brothers, you did it to me" (Matthew 25:40). The people God brings into our lives, especially the people we meet at church, are given to us to connect us to him, all while God uses us in the lives of those same people to help them connect with God. C. S. Lewis saw this clearly:

> We are summoned from the outset to combine as creatures with our Creator, as mortals with immortal, as redeemed sinners with sinless Redeemer. His presence, the interaction between Him and us, must always be the overwhelmingly dominant factor in the life we are to lead within the Body, and any conception of Christian fellowship which does not mean primarily fellowship with Him is out of court.[41]

---

[41]C. S. Lewis, "Membership" in *The Weight of Glory and Other Addresses* (New York, NY: Harper Collins, 2001), 166. If you're thinking that your experience in church doesn't really match the description you just read, I understand. I have had that same kind of

DEEP PRAYER

When we go to church, and someone gently corrects (or harshly rebukes) us for a sin he thinks we might be struggling with, it's easy to get offended and defensive. What if, instead, you saw him as being used by God to speak to you? Then you would be spurred on to examine your soul and study the Bible to see if he is right, to see if you're blind to something. Even if you figure out that he is wrong, you will have had a conversation with God about something important in your life and still may have seen something you were unaware of.

Someone at church could also thank you or praise you for something you've done, or encourage you in something you're doing. When you hear that, it's easy to shrink back, to think you don't deserve it, and to fear becoming proud. What if, instead, you see this praise or encouragement as God speaking to you? Then you can talk to him about it, whether this was empty flattery or you really were helpful, whether you're tempted to do other things for the praise of men, and you can ask him to keep you from pride as you realize that you did what you did in the strength God gave you. This process might even help you to see areas of ministry where you can be effective and could be God's way

---

disappointing experience in more than one church in my lifetime. That's the reality when sinners gather together inside a sinful world. On top of that, churches tend to reflect the culture they are sitting in, so it should come as no surprise that we see shriveled up relationships within churches that operate in a culture filled with shriveled up relationships.

The Conversation of Deep Prayer

of letting you know that this is the ministry he has designed for you.

Repeated Prayer Without an Answer

Many times, we pray deep prayers that ask God to do something about a burden we're carrying, and we get no answer at all. This has happened to me more times than I can count. It even happens when I am regularly listening to God through his Word. Nothing I hear, as I make my way through the Bible day by day, helps me with my burden. What should we do when this happens?

Keep praying and keep listening.

I have mentioned Paul's thorn in the flesh before, how Paul prayed that God would remove his thorn, but God told him he would not remove it; instead, he would give him grace to live with it, even be thankful for it. But let's look at it again:

> So to keep me from becoming conceited because of the surpassing greatness of the revelations, a thorn was given me in the flesh, a messenger of Satan to harass me, to keep me from becoming conceited. Three times I pleaded with the Lord about this, that it should leave me (2 Corinthians 12:7-8).

Notice that Paul "pleaded with the Lord about this" but God didn't answer him right away. Paul told the Corinthians that it wasn't until he had pleaded with the Lord the third time that God spoke to him about his thorn. Why did Paul pray three times? After all, Paul was a great apostle who received massive revelations from God about all kinds of things. Shouldn't Paul have accepted God's silence as his answer and just accepted the thorn wasn't going to be removed?

That's exactly the point. This thorn was a burden to Paul—a physical burden, of course, but also a burden on his soul and a hardship to his ministry. That's why he kept asking that it be removed. It's even possible that Paul's three prayers corresponded to three times when the thorn's attack on his flesh was most severe, so that the pain Paul felt moved him to ask God to take it away.[42] When the pain eased, Paul was able to pray about other things and go on with his ministry. But when the pain came back, Paul didn't hesitate to pray the same prayer again, asking the Lord to remove the thorn from his flesh.

I'm sure you have family members who you've been praying would be saved—maybe for decades—maybe without seeing any movement in their lives toward God. They might even be plunging deeper into sin as you pray for their souls. I'm sure you have certain sins that attack you relentlessly, and you have repented and asked God to remove them over and over. You have probably faced trials where

---

[42]Murray J. Harris, *The Second Epistle to the Corinthians: A Commentary on the Greek Text* (Grand Rapids, MI, William B. Eerdmans Publishing Company, 2005), 861.

The Conversation of Deep Prayer

you cried out to God without seeing any kind of answer. What should you do? Follow Paul's example and keep praying the same prayer over and over again as long as your soul is burdened with these needs and troubles. Paul was unique, and we are not Paul. However, his situation isn't unique at all, and we can respond the way Paul did when we pray and nothing seems to happen.

I started this chapter by exhorting you not to do all the talking in your conversations with God—to listen to God as you're also talking to him—and now I'm using Paul's example to tell you what to do when God isn't talking. I realize that may be confusing, but I can explain. First, God is still talking, he is just not addressing the very thing that's burdening you at the moment. You need to keep listening because what he is saying to you may be preparing you to hear what he has to say later. Second, don't stop praying about what burdens you. Yes, Paul stopped asking God to *remove* his thorn after three prayers, but I seriously doubt Paul stopped talking to God *about* his thorn, even after God told him what he was doing. The thorn was still there, still causing physical pain, still getting in the way of his ministry; but instead of asking God to remove it, I'm sure Paul prayed for the grace and strength God had told him he would give Paul along with the thorn. Third, never assume that God isn't working, both on you and on your burdens.

DEEP PRAYER

At the end of Exodus, chapter 2, while all the descendants of Abraham were enslaved to the Egyptians, their prayer for deliverance is recorded:

> During those many days the king of Egypt died, and the people of Israel groaned because of their slavery and cried out for help. Their cry for rescue from slavery came up to God. And God heard their groaning, and God remembered his covenant with Abraham, with Isaac, and with Jacob. God saw the people of Israel—and God knew (Exodus 2:23-25).

This text foreshadows God's actions in the book of Exodus by telling us that God heard, God remembered, God saw, and God knew about the burdens his people were living under. Although that sounds encouraging, the slaves in Egypt could see none of that, and their lives were just as horrible as ever. They still got up every morning to work hard under the whips of their task masters. But, on the other side of the desert, God was about to speak to Moses, commission him as his emissary, and send him back to Egypt to free the people from their slavery. This part of the story starts in verse 1 of chapter 3—the very next verse after the Israelites cried out in prayer. God was already working on the answer to that prayer even though the people groaning in prayer couldn't see what he was doing.

The same may be true of you: God may be on the far side of the desert preparing your deliverance while you're crying out to God and feeling frustrated that he hasn't answered. Never take God's silence as rejection or indifference.

The Conversation of Deep Prayer

Instead, keep praying deep prayers, keep listening deeply to God's Word, and wait for his answer.

Deep prayers are conversations not soliloquies. But they are not aimless, meandering conversations, moving along without any direction. When God speaks to us, he has a purpose, an aim, a goal, an end in mind. Every conversation we have with God is going somewhere. When we have these conversations of deep prayer, God is moving us closer and closer to praying the one prayer that he guarantees he will always answer. It's the prayer Jesus taught his disciples to pray: "Your will be done on earth as it is in heaven" (Matthew 6:10). It's also the prayer Jesus eventually prayed while lying on his face in Gethsemane: "nevertheless, not as I will, but as you will" (Matthew 26:39). That's the lesson of the next chapter.

CHAPTER 7

THE END OF DEEP PRAYER

One beautiful, sunny day, eight-year-old Billy asked his mother if he could go out in the yard to play. His mom's answer surprised him. "No, Billy, not today." Billy had been looking out the window all through breakfast and knew the weather was great, better than it was yesterday when he played out in the yard all morning. To his young mind, his mother's refusal made no sense at all, so he looked up at her and asked, "Why not?"

As it turned out, Billy's mom had a really good reason to keep Billy inside that day. She had information that Billy didn't have, information that Billy couldn't even understand. When Billy asked her why he couldn't go out to play on such a beautiful day, she couldn't tell him all the reasons that brought her to that decision, so she just told Billy that he had to trust her, that she knew what was best for him, and that she had her reasons. But Billy loved playing outside so, instead of accepting his mom's decision, he did what kids do: he had himself a little tantrum, whining about the unfairness of it all, complaining about how bored he was in the house, arguing that there was no reason he was being forced to stay inside. None of this, however, changed his mother's mind. She was protecting him when she said no that day; she was loving him when she said no that day; she was caring for him when she said no that day. Nothing Billy said or did would make her stop protecting or loving or caring for him. The relationship between Billy and his mom was a little strained that day, but Billy was safe and he soon got over his tantrum and felt his mother's love once again.

Parents have to say no to their kids every day because their kids don't know things that the parents know; because their kids think only about the short-term benefits of what they want and ignore the long-term consequences; because their kids care more about having fun and don't think at all about developing a mature character. Parents say no to their children because they love them deeply and want what's best for them in life. They may refuse their children's requests but they never reject their children. Parents also have to say "No" to their kids because hearing that word helps children grow up into responsible adults. Study after study has shown that, when kids are given everything they want, when parents confuse love with gratification and indulgence, those kids grow up unable to function in the world, unprepared for the hardships they will inevitably face as adults, unable to plan for the future, incapable of denying themselves even harmful pleasures, and unwilling to give to others since all their relationships are based on what they can get for themselves.

Children who grow up with parents who love them truly, deeply, and wisely, are greatly blessed by how they were raised and, as they become adults, they learn that there was great value in hearing the world "No" on a regular basis, by not getting their way all the time, by being guided by a far deeper love than their own self-love and a far more superior will than their own selfish will.

From the Lesser to the Greater

Our Father in heaven is the perfect parent: greater and more loving than any human parent could ever be. His love is more consistent, his will is perfect, and his wisdom is infinite. He has committed himself to our eternal blessing and happiness, so he refuses to give us anything that will harm us or damage our souls. If you're able to accept that a child benefits when his earthly parents guide him according to their love and wisdom, you should enthusiastically agree there must be an even greater blessing for your soul when your heavenly Father guides you with his infinite love and perfect wisdom.

In fact, if you think about it for just a couple of minutes, you should choose God's will over your own will every time you pray. The prayers, "Your will be done" and "not as I will but as you will," should be the easiest words for you to pray. After all, God knows everything, "declaring the end from the beginning" (Isaiah 46:10); he has unlimited power, doing "whatever he pleases" (Psalm 115:3); he is the personification of wisdom (Proverbs 8) and is called "the only wise God" (Romans 16:27). More than that, "God is love" (1 John 4:8, 16) and works "all things . . . together for good" for those who love him (Romans 8:28). When we surrender our own will and submit to God's, we're not submitting to blind fate or merely obeying someone too strong to fight; we're trusting the one who loves us most, who has perfect wisdom, who knows everything, and can do anything. Plus, the will we're surrendering—our own will—is infected by our sinful souls, is warped by our limited knowledge, and applies wisdom so defective we should call it folly. Why would anyone hang on to his own will when he can have God's will?

From Knowledge to Practice

Unfortunately for us, it's not that easy to throw aside our own will and embrace the perfect wisdom and infinite love found in God's will. Why? Because we don't cling to our own will on the strength of truth or logic or reason, but on something far more powerful: our passions and desires.

A little girl, growing up in a Christian home and going to a good church, decides at a young age that she wants to get married when she grows up. She sees the happiness of her parents, she observes that most of the adults in her church are married, she reads in the Bible that God created marriage and made it an important step in the progression of life (Genesis 2:24). As she enters her 20's, she desires marriage as a good thing and is sure that marriage is God's will for her.

What if it turns out that God's will for this young woman is to remain single for her entire life? What if the God who has all wisdom, the Father who knows her best, the Savior who loves her most, chooses a single life for her? How hard will it be for her to give up her own will to follow God's? It will be an agonizing journey. First, God's plan will never be completely clear to her. Just because she hasn't married by age 30 doesn't mean she will never marry. Second, she cannot frame the issue as choosing her will over God's. She has already decided that marriage must be God's will and abandoning marriage means rebellion, not submission, to God's plan. Third, her desire to be married has created an expectation in her life that shapes her idea of what her life should be. When that expectation isn't met, she feels that she has somehow failed to get the best life that God had promised her. Even if she could intellectually assent to singleness being God's will, she may always feel like something is missing. Her will is so ingrained in her soul that when she prays, "not my will but yours be done," in her mind she is asking God to send her a husband.

It's not just single women who have this struggle. All Christians who develop a deep desire for something good in their life will struggle just like that young woman if it turns out they are pursuing their will, not God's. The couple who got married with a strong love and desire for children but who are still childless after a decade of trying. The man who grew up in a poverty that fueled his passion to get out of that ghetto and be successful, but who God is calling into a thankless, low-paying ministry back in his old neighborhood. The woman who was sure God wanted her to have an important profession, like a doctor or a lawyer, but ends up pouring herself (and her great education) into her six children every day. The Christian who had plans to spend retirement around family and doing ministry but is told that all those tests recently taken have revealed terminal cancer.

Notice that none of the things these Christians want is sinful or wrong; they are not even strange or unusual. But, when something like this gets deep into our soul, we think we want God's will; we never imagine that it's really our own will that we're clinging to and pursuing. We have convinced ourselves we're following God's path and plan for our life.

So, even if we can accept, in theory, that giving up our selfish and foolish will and embracing God's wise and loving will for our life is an immense blessing for our souls, we still struggle, in practice, to choose God's will and surrender our own will. We need God's work in our souls to move us in the right direction one step at a time. This step-by-step process toward submitting to God's will is the goal, the end, of deep prayer. When we use the honest and open language of deep prayer to talk to God about everything in our lives, and we receive the blessing of a closer relationship with God through those prayers, and we engage God in a conversation, listening to him as he teaches and leads us, the end of all of this is that we will be able to submit to his will for our life.

Actually, "submit" isn't the right word. We can submit out of necessity with rebellion in our hearts. We can add words like, "nevertheless, not as I will, but as you will" to the end of our prayers without really meaning it. What our Father is doing when we pray these deep prayers is revealing enough of himself to us until we prefer the Father's will more than our own; until we value the Father's will above our own; until we desire the Father's will instead of our own. When we're drawn into this kind of intimate relationship, we will eventually add the words, "not as I will, but as you will" to our prayers, not as a punchline, but as a true expression of our heart's desire.

Back to the Garden

This, of course, is exactly what happened to Jesus. In his conversation with his Father, Jesus got to the point (three times) where he could say, "not as I will but as you will" (Matthew 26:39, 42, 44). The will that Jesus embraced was his Father's will to save souls by sending Jesus to hang alone on the cross, enduring a pain far greater than the physical torture of a crucifixion. Even after embracing his Father's will, even after walking straight through the arrest and trial and indignity of carrying his cross up the hill, Jesus was still

The End of Deep Prayer

in great pain and he cried out, in the words of Psalm 22:1, "My God, my God, why have you forsaken me?" (Matthew 27:46).

It's easy to say that the Father abandoned his beloved Son to die because it was the will of God that his death save sinners and, over the 20 centuries since the cross, we have seen the gospel preached around the world and millions upon millions of sinners saved by his bloody sacrifice. But there is more to it than just that. The Father let his Son hang alone on that cross not only because that's what is best for all us sinners, but also because that was the Father's perfect path toward Jesus's highest goal, a goal so great and so high, we have to go up to heaven to see it.

In Revelation 5, God gave Jesus's beloved apostle, John, a vision of heaven, where he stood before the throne of God and saw a scroll in God's right hand. Then he heard a mighty angel proclaim in a loud voice, "Who is worthy to open the scroll and break its seals?" (Revelation 5:2). This honor was so high, that no one—in heaven, on earth, and even under the earth—was deemed worthy (v. 3). John, recognizing the importance of getting this scroll opened, began to weep when he heard the verdict of universal unworthiness (v. 4). But then one of the elders sitting around God's throne said to John, "Weep no more; behold, the Lion of the tribe of Judah, the Root of David, has conquered, so that he can open the scroll and its seven seals" (v. 5). We know this is Jesus because, in verse 6, he is described as "a Lamb standing, as though it had been slain."

We read this and think, "Of course Jesus is worthy! He is the second person of the Trinity, God of God, of one nature with the Father and the Spirit! He exists eternally in himself while everyone else is created by him. He stands alone." And that's all true. John told us, "In the beginning was the Word [Jesus], and the Word was with God, and the Word was God" (John 1:1); Paul called him "God over all" (Romans 9:5); and the book of Hebrews proclaims Jesus to be "the radiance of the glory of God and the exact imprint of his nature . . . [who] upholds the universe by the word of his power" (Hebrews 1:3). Jesus possesses, in his nature as God, a transcendent and eternal glory independent of anything that happened on this earth. You would think that all this would make him worthy to do anything, including snapping open those seven seals and reading the words on that scroll.

But the elder didn't say that Jesus was worthy because he is God; the elder said Jesus was worthy because he had *conquered*, because he went to the cross. As Jesus took the scroll, the four living creatures and the twenty-four elders fell down before him and started singing a new song:

> Worthy are you to take the scroll and to open its seals,
> *for you were slain, and by your blood you ransomed people for God*

The End of Deep Prayer

> *from every tribe and language and people and nation,*
> and you have made them a kingdom and priests to our God,
> and they shall reign on the earth (Revelation 5:9-10).

Jesus was worthy to open this particular scroll because he died on the cross and because his death saved sinners. This chorus wasn't sung by some fringe group in a forgotten backwater who were confused about Jesus's divine nature, this was the new song sung by the twenty-four elders and the four living creatures who live in the presence of God himself. And their song says that Jesus was worthy to open this scroll because the Father refused, even in the face of Jesus's deep and desperate prayer in the garden that night, to abandon his will for his beloved Son.

John wasn't the only apostle to see heaven. Paul was given a glimpse into that world once, either in a vision or in his physical body (he wasn't sure about that himself; see 2 Corinthians 12:2-4), and he came back with the same message about Jesus. When he wrote to the Philippian church, he pointed them to Jesus as a model of humility to follow:

> Have this mind among yourselves, which is yours in Christ Jesus, who, though he was in the form of God, did not count equality with God a thing to be grasped, but emptied himself, by taking the form of a servant, being born in the likeness of men. And being found in human

form, he humbled himself by becoming obedient to the point of death, even death on a cross (Philippians 2:5-8).

Since Paul put Jesus forward as the model to follow here, he made Jesus the subject of all the verbs in the sentence: *Jesus* emptied himself, *Jesus* took the form of a servant, *Jesus* was born in the likeness of men, *Jesus* humbled himself, *Jesus* was obedient all the way to the cross. Then, after holding Jesus up as an example, Paul told the Philippians what happened to Jesus up in heaven because he died on the cross:

> *Therefore* God has highly exalted him and bestowed on him the name that is above every name, so that at the name of Jesus every knee should bow, in heaven and on earth and under the earth, and every tongue confess that Jesus Christ is Lord, to the glory of God the Father. (Philippians 2:9-11).

Since Paul is now telling us what happened to Jesus, Jesus isn't the subject of this sentence, the Father is. Paul is describing what the Father has done for Jesus: *God* has highly exalted him; *God* has bestowed on him the highest name; *God* makes every knee bow to Jesus and every tongue confess that he is Lord. But the key word in this passage is the first word: Therefore. Everything the Father did to Jesus was done because Jesus humbled himself all the way to the cross. The link to the previous passage is strong—the humbling acts of Jesus are the very reason the Father exalted him. It's grammatically impossible for this hymn of

The End of Deep Prayer

exaltation to stand alone, as if Jesus has his name and position in himself, simply because he is, by nature, God. Paul forces us to conclude that this exaltation is the direct result of Jesus's obedience to his Father's will—as he said in the garden, "nevertheless, not as I will but as you will" (Matthew 26:39).

As Jesus prayed for relief from the agony that was about to engulf him, the Father's deep love and infinite wisdom kept him on that dark path because that was the path to his exaltation. Every time a broken sinner runs to Jesus for salvation, or a grateful Christian thanks Jesus for bearing his sins, or a church sings praises to Jesus for being the Savior of the world, the Father's plan is vindicated. When Peter stood before the Jewish leaders and said, "And there is salvation in no one else, for there is *no other name under heaven given among men* by which we must be saved" (Acts 4:12); when Paul wrote, "since we have been justified by faith, we have peace with God *through our Lord Jesus Christ*" (Romans 5:1); every time Jesus is called the head of the church (Ephesians 1:22, 5:23; Colossians 1:18); when Jesus tells us we can do nothing apart from him (John 15:4-5); when Paul tells us we can do all things through him (Philippians 4:13); and whenever we read in the Bible that everything we have, we have "in Christ" (Ephesians 1:3), the love and wisdom of the Father shines brightly and we finally see the immeasurable blessing in Jesus's one and only unanswered prayer.

DEEP PRAYER

The end of Jesus's deep prayer in the garden was that Jesus embraced and experienced the fullness of the Father's will in his exaltation in heaven for all eternity. The Father refused Jesus's prayer not because he was cruel, not because he was callous about the ordeal Jesus was about to face, not even because he cared more about saving sinners than he did about the suffering of his Son, but because, in his wisdom, his plan made Jesus the focal point of world history, the center of every Christian life, and the object of our grateful worship.

The Wise Love of God Working in Deep Prayers

We can see this same wise love in our own deep prayers every time God leads us away from our own will so we can embrace and experience his will for us. And just like Jesus, the full blessing of God's plan can only be seen when we get to heaven. It turns out that the end of all your deep prayers—the answered and the unanswered—is a straight road through life, the road that takes you to God in heaven.

If you're thinking that this cannot be true because you're not Jesus and so the Father doesn't treat you the same way, then you're completely wrong. Listen to what Jesus asked his Father to do for you in his great prayer during the Last

The End of Deep Prayer

Supper:[43] "I made known to them your name, and I will continue to make it known, that *the love with which you have loved me may be in them*, and I in them" (John 17:26).[44] Jesus wanted to make his Father's name known to all his disciples across time specifically so that the Father's love for Jesus could be experienced by each of us. The Father loves you like he loves Jesus. The Father's end for all your deep prayers is the same for you as it was for Jesus's deepest prayer—for you to experience the blessing and glory of the wise, loving, perfect will of your Father for all eternity.

This is another reason why deep prayer isn't a gimmick, it's a relationship. We don't pray deep prayers to manipulate God into doing our will, we pray deep prayers so we can desire God's will. Our deep prayers pull us closer to our Father as he speaks to us through the Bible, shows us his love and wisdom, and increases our love for him. This often takes time.

Let's consider what that process might look like by revisiting our 30-year-old single woman who has been

---

[43] In John 17:20, Jesus said, "I do not ask for these only, but also for those who will believe in me through their word." From verse 20 through the end of the prayer Jesus is praying for all the Christians who have come after his original twelve disciples, including you.

[44] He prayed something similar a couple of verses earlier: "The glory that you have given me I have given to them, that they may be one even as we are one, I in them and you in me, that they may become perfectly one, so that the world may know that you sent me and *loved them even as you loved me*" (verses 22-23, emphasis added).

planning her wedding since she was fifteen. At some point, as she makes her way through her twenties, she may start to become anxious, or even fearful, that she still hasn't met the man God wants her to marry. So, she starts to talk to God about this in the language of deep prayer—openness, honesty, authenticity, and frankness. Depending on her personality, these deep prayers may sound like a complaint or a lament; or they might express disappointment and frustration; or they might cry out with insecurity as she wonders if God has abandoned her; or she may even lash out in anger at her situation.

Then, through her deep prayer, her Father will begin to work in her soul and talk to her as she takes in the message of the Bible. As God speaks to her and teaches her and draws her closer to himself, it's possible that none of it will bear directly on her desire to be married. It's more likely that God will be working on why she feels sad or disappointed or frustrated or insecure or angry. Over time, he will show her how much he loves her and how deep his wisdom is; he may show her that she can trust him for anything and that he desires what's best for her. In this process, her love for her Father and for her Betrothed will grow into deeper intimacy which will help her abandon some of her sin and correct her attitudes about life. He may even give her a life full of responsibility and a fulfilling ministry in her church. At some point along this journey, whenever she prays about finding a husband and getting married, she is able to sincerely say, "Nevertheless, not my will but yours be done."

This is the end of deep prayer and will be a wonderful blessing to her soul, but the fullness of God's wise and loving plan for her will not be known until she gets to heaven and sees the impact her life had on the people around her and the ways the kingdom of heaven was advanced in the world because she bore the responsibilities she was given and took seriously the ministries that opened up to her. In heaven, she will look back at her singleness and not see a cruel hardship, but the beautiful and blessed road that carried her straight to God in heaven.

Objection: Not Everyone Has a Happy Ending

You might be looking at this rosy picture I just painted and be thinking that this isn't right, that even Christians die alone and forgotten, in pain and in grief. Like the man living in a Muslim or Communist country who, after a long struggle to believe, confesses his sin and trusts in Jesus, only to be arrested a couple of days later, thrown in prison for the rest of his life, and eventually killed in isolation, neglect, and torture. Or like the woman who faithfully served her church for decades until she lost her physical strength and became a shut-in, only to be eventually forgotten and ignored by her own church. Do stories like that have the happy ending I described?

Absolutely. The moment a person is adopted into God's family, his story is no longer tied to this earth or limited by time, so we cannot evaluate the ending by looking only at his or her life on earth. God's wisdom and love take a much, much longer view than the short blip of time we have here on earth. Whatever God is doing in the lives of the people who die in pain or loneliness or grief will be carried into heaven with them and become part of the happiest of endings.

That's our final lesson from the book of Job. All the times I have mentioned Job previously in this book, I have always pointed to his trial, grief and, especially, his deep prayers. But Job's story had such a ridiculously happy ending it almost sounds like a fairy tale:

> And the LORD restored the fortunes of Job, when he had prayed for his friends. And the LORD gave Job twice as much as he had before. Then came to him all his brothers and sisters and all who had known him before, and ate bread with him in his house. And they showed him sympathy and comforted him for all the evil that the LORD had brought upon him. And each of them gave him a piece of money and a ring of gold.
> And the LORD blessed the latter days of Job more than his beginning. And he had 14,000 sheep, 6,000 camels, 1,000 yoke of oxen, and 1,000 female donkeys. He had also seven sons and three daughters. And he called the name of the first daughter Jemimah, and the name of the second Keziah, and the name of the third Keren-happuch. And in all the land there were no women so beautiful as Job's daughters. And their father gave them an inheritance among their brothers. And after this Job lived 140 years, and saw his sons, and his sons' sons,

four generations. And Job died, an old man, and full of days (Job 42:10-17).

Job lost three significant blessings in his trial: his community, as everyone he knew abandoned him while he suffered; his wealth, which was either stolen or destroyed; and his children, who were all killed. But as the story comes to a close, he gets all three of these back. First, the people who abandoned him came back and blessed him (v. 11). Second, the Lord blessed him with double the wealth he had before (v. 10). Finally, he had ten children, the same number he had lost and in same combination of sons and daughters (v. 13).

Some interpreters believe that this ending actually is a fairy tale, that it was added long after the book was written, perhaps by someone who couldn't live without a happy ending to the story. They have a point, too. All through the book, Job's three friends told him that if he would only repent of whatever sin caused God to make him suffer, God would forgive him and restore him. Then, Job repented (42:6) and God gave him his life back. The fairy tale ending, they say, undermines the message of the book.

I disagree. First, because Job didn't repent of the undefined sins his friends were pushing him to confess, he repented of his small and incomplete view of God that was revealed to him when God finally spoke. Second, I think God is showing us, by blessing Job so overwhelmingly at the end of the book, a picture of heaven, a picture of the blessing every Christian will experience when his or her life on earth ends.

The greatest blessing of heaven is God himself. Heaven is where our relationship with God moves from faith to sight and we finally get to look on his beautiful face. That's exactly what Job said he received at the end of his trial: "I had heard of you by the hearing of the ear, but now my eye sees you" (Job 42:5). For Job this was a metaphor for a growing relationship with God, but for us, it will be literally true that we will look upon our invisible Father and the glorified Jesus.

While we're in heaven, in the glorious presence of the Triune God, we will notice others around the throne, our community of believers who were separated from us during our life, either by death or circumstances or geography. We will have a newer, sweeter fellowship with them. We will also be blessed with greater wealth than we have ever known. I don't mean the wealth of having a pile of gold stored in the basement of your huge mansion, I mean the wealth of having every need and every desire met, wanting for nothing while living in never-ending bliss. Finally, we will be reunited with parents and children, wives and husbands. While I'm pretty sure the blood relationships we have on earth will be different in heaven, I also think some part of those relationships will still exist. I find it interesting that Job didn't just have the same number of children, he had the same number of sons and the same number of daughters. If we read this as a story of heaven, this feels more like a reunion with the children who got there before him than a set of replacement children. After all, you can replace a sheep with another sheep or a camel with another camel, but not a child with another child.

This is how your story is going to end. No matter how much you've suffered (or will suffer), no matter what trials you've endured (or will endure), no matter how tragic your life has been (or will still be), you not only get a happy ending, but an eternal and glorious ending. Whenever God refuses to answer one of your deep prayers to end that suffering or to put you on a different road, he is keeping you on the path of his perfect will that leads to your ultimate blessing.

Heaven's Perspective on Earthly Suffering

Paul suffered greatly in his life, but he always saw his suffering from a heavenly perspective. For example, in 1 Corinthians 15, Paul wrote about the resurrection from the dead, both Christ's resurrection and ours as followers of Christ. It's an amazing chapter that makes a powerful argument that the resurrection of Jesus guarantees that we will be resurrected, that our resurrection will be physical, and that this physical resurrection will be glorious. But nestled among all that glory, Paul managed to slip in an important application connecting the future resurrection of

Christians to their present suffering in this world when he wrote, "If in Christ we have hope in this life only, we are of all people most to be pitied" (v. 19). If our stories don't end in heaven, then we're all a bunch of fools and our pain and grief isn't the wise love of God in action, it's just a lot of pain and a lot of grief. But Paul's argument is that all our stories will end in heaven, and that changes everything.

When Paul wrote to the Corinthians again later, he expanded on this connection between suffering in this life and the glorious ending of our stories. In 2 Corinthians 4, he wrote about the hardships of the ministry in light of the glory of heaven:

> But we have this treasure in jars of clay, to show that the surpassing power belongs to God and not to us. We are afflicted in every way, but not crushed; perplexed, but not driven to despair; persecuted, but not forsaken; struck down, but not destroyed; always carrying in the body the death of Jesus, so that the life of Jesus may also be manifested in our bodies. For we who live are always being given over to death for Jesus' sake, so that the life of Jesus also may be manifested in our mortal flesh. So death is at work in us, but life in you (vv. 7-12).

You can hear in this testimony that, although his hardships were real, difficult, and painful, they weren't ultimate for Paul. That's why, just a few verses later, he could write,

> So we do not lose heart. Though our outer self is wasting away, our inner self is being renewed day by

The End of Deep Prayer

day. *For this light momentary affliction is preparing for us an eternal weight of glory beyond all comparison*, as we look not to the things that are seen but to the things that are unseen. For the things that are seen are transient, but the things that are unseen are eternal (vv. 16-18).

The suffering, which seems to last too long and weigh on us so much, will be considered both light and momentary as soon as we see the eternal glory of heaven. Paul wrote something similar to the Romans: "For I consider that the sufferings of this present time are not worth comparing to the glory that is to be revealed to us" (Romans 8:18). It's not just that the glory will be greater than the suffering, but that it's so much greater, it's foolish to even compare them at all—but not in the way we shouldn't compare apples and oranges, but more like comparing gold with rubbish. It's not worth the effort.

As encouraging as that is, Paul told the Romans something else about suffering and glory. He said that, just like Jesus's exaltation came through the cross, so our only path to glory is through our suffering: "The Spirit himself bears witness with our spirit that we are children of God, and if children, then heirs—heirs of God and fellow heirs with Christ, *provided we suffer with him in order that we may also be glorified with him*" (Romans 8:16-17).

It sounds like Paul is saying that, although the road to heaven takes us though suffering, hardship, sickness, pain, and separation, the final destination makes it worth the trip.

DEEP PRAYER

And he is saying at least this, but C. S. Lewis thinks Paul is saying even more. In a strange, allegorical book called, *The Great Divorce*, Lewis has one of his characters (a person living in heaven) explain it this way: "That is what mortals misunderstand. They say of some temporal suffering, 'No future bliss can make up for it,' not knowing that Heaven, once attained, will work backwards and turn even that agony into a glory."[45] Suffering isn't just what we endure to get to heaven, it's actually the highway we travel that brings us to heaven. Once we get there, the suffering will not be worth comparing to the glory we see because the suffering itself will become part of that glory! As we look back along that glorious road, we will not see the pain, hardships, trials, difficulties, and losses we endured as we walked down that path. We will see the footprints of Jesus, we will see the depth of our relationship with the Father, we will see how our souls were freed from sin, we will see all the fruit of the ministry that grew out of our hardships, and we will see the connections we forged with other Christians along the way, plus lots of other things produced by those trials that will shine so brightly we will be blinded by the glory of it all.

And that's the end of deep prayer.

---

[45] C. S. Lewis, *The Great Divorce*, The Centenary Press (London, 1945), 62.

A CALL TO DEEP PRAYER

I wrote this book to encourage Christians to pray deep prayers to God regularly and intentionally. In deep prayer, you open yourself up to your Father and your betrothed while your human spirit connects with the indwelling Spirit of God. Through your deep prayers, you listen to God and get to know him much more intimately. As you pray your deep prayers, your love for God grows while your love for your sins diminishes. Deep prayers strengthen your soul for whatever you have to face, whether overwhelming blessings or life-altering trials, so you can walk with your best friend on any road he takes you down. In deep prayer, you learn to ask more from God while you're constantly receiving more of God.

Of course, just reading this book will not do any of that in your life; you have to actually pray! So, now that you have read this book, I want to encourage you one last time to pray deep prayers to God regularly and intentionally. The greatest gift that God has given you is the relationship he pursues with you—as your Father, as your betrothed, and as the indwelling Spirit. I'm asking you to regularly and intentionally pray deep prayers so you can experience the overwhelming joy, the constant comfort, the amazing grace, the wonderful freedom, the real righteousness, the spiritual strength, the inner courage, and the breathtaking delight that only come inside your intimate relationship with your God.

I'm not calling you to merely say your prayers every day or have your quiet time more consistently. I'm calling you to pray deep prayers regularly and intentionally until you can say to God, like Job did, "I had heard of you by the hearing of the ear, but now my eye sees you" (Job 42:5); until you know the "love of Christ that surpasses knowledge" and you're "filled with all the fullness of God" (Ephesians 3:19); until you can cry out "Abba! Father!" in your hardest trials and sharpest pain (Mark 14:36); until you can say, with joy, "nevertheless not as I will, but as you will" (Matthew 26:39).

The Christian church today needs Christians who know their God like this, who can talk to their God like this. I became a Christian in 1973. Over the more than half a century since then, I have watched, year after year, Western culture move further and further from its Christian roots to embrace sin, evil, and even death. I have watched, over and over again, sins that were on the fringe of society, hidden in the shadows and shrouded in shame, slowly move out of the darkness and into the full light of day. To accommodate these sins, righteousness that once held a place of honor, has been driven out to the fringes. In the resulting turmoil, many, many Christians have been caught up in the culture and been snared by these sins—sometimes before coming to Jesus and sometimes after. Although these sins have been nailed to the cross and forgiven forever, we still have to fight against and struggle with these culturally acceptable sins.

A Call to Deep Prayer

Divorce, once a rare and shameful failure, is now normal and routine, one of the expectations of marriage. Abortion, once illegal in most of the United States and restricted in all of them, was made legal by judicial fiat and has become a form of birth control. Homosexuality, once considered a sin by the church and a mental illness by psychiatrists, is now proudly celebrated as a birthright. Pornography, once considered the haunt of perverts who exploited women, can now delivered to every computer, smartphone, and tablet in the world and is treated as normal. Marriage, once a solemn covenant between a man and a woman and revered as the cornerstone of a stable society, is now criticized as a vestige of the oppressive patriarchy, where women are enslaved and raped, and has become a temporary contract of convenience between any two people. Children, once protected from violence, evil, and sexualization, are now exposed to it all in schools, on television, in movies, and on social media. Education, once the place where diverse options were examined to find the truth, is now the place where speech is shut down to facilitate indoctrination. Businesses, once (mostly) left alone to succeed or fail to meet the needs of their customers, are now used as instruments to push social agendas and subsidized to make products unpopular with consumers but demanded by government. Politicians, once respected as local and national leaders, now work hard to protect and prosper themselves rather than their constituents. And government at all levels, federal, state, and even local, continue to spend recklessly, foolishly, and corruptly, racking up more public debt than can be paid back over the next three or four generations.

Meanwhile, churches across the West have shown a tendency to drift with the current right along with the culture, many putting a higher value on relevance than on faithfulness. Thankfully, God has reserved for himself many pastors, theologians, leaders, and laymen who have not bowed the knee to the culture, but far, far too many find excuses to go along or are blindly unaware of the dangers facing the church. Church members are often not confronted with or taught about the sins around them and, when they are, are more likely to ignore this teaching than respond to it.

We live in a culture that is actively pursuing its own destruction and we need Christians from all walks of life to stand against this onslaught, to show the glory of God in their daily lives, to be faithful witnesses of the truth being denied all around us. We desperately need a movement of the Spirit of God, a revival in which millions of souls are saved, that pours common grace out all around the world, that brings light into our current darkness and breathes life into our culture of death. Unfortunately, I'm not sure our churches are ready for that kind of movement by the Spirit; I don't think we could handle it. So, that's also part of my call to prayer.

A Call to Deep Prayer

All the things God does in the individual soul who prays deep prayers regularly and intentionally, will be multiplied exponentially as those Christians gather together in local churches, serving one another, loving one another, confronting one another, and—especially—praying with one another. I have no idea if God will send us the revival we seek, but I do know that we desperately need Christians who know their God intimately and who connect themselves to other Christians who also know God intimately. Then, if God sends us a revival, we will be ready for it and, if he doesn't, we will be ready for that, too.

I close this book with the final words from J. C. Ryle's *A Call to Prayer* from a century and a half ago. I find in these words (with some slight modifications) an expression of my own heart:

> I want the times we live in to be praying times. I want the Christians of our day to be praying Christians. I want the church of our age to be a praying church. My heart's desire and prayer in sending out this publication is to promote a spirit of prayerfulness. I want those who have never yet prayed to rise and call upon God; and I want those who do pray, to [deepen] their prayers every year, and see that they are not becoming slack [by] praying in [a shallow] way.[46]

---

[46]J. C. Ryle, *Practical Religion* (Auburn, MA, Evangelical Press, 2001), 106.

EPILOGUE

This book is not a theological treatise on all the Bible has to say about prayer. The goal of this book has been to show you the reason prayer exists—the reason God calls us into this remarkable conversation with him—and then to encourage you to pray according to that purpose regularly and intentionally. As a result of this focus, you may be disappointed that I didn't discuss your favorite prayer or your favorite verse about prayer.

I'm sorry about that but I hope I have given you a tool that you can use to see that favorite prayer or passage with new understanding. So, you can read the prayer of Moses for the nation of Israel and hear his concern for God's glory and his ability to talk to God frankly and openly. You will feel the pain in Hannah's prayer as she begs God to give her a son and remove her shame. You will recognize, as Solomon prays at the dedication of the temple, his authentic praise and sincere joy that God will dwell with his people. You will hear, throughout the book of Psalms, the vast array of emotions expressed and the deeply personal ways people talk to God. You will be amazed at the depth of Paul's relationship with God as he prays for church after church, seeking their highest good and greatest joy in knowing God themselves. And, of course, you will see the intimacy of Jesus with his Father every time he prays, even when the words are not recorded.

www.ingramcontent.com/pod-product-compliance
Lightning Source LLC
Chambersburg PA
CBHW031640040426
42453CB00006B/160